Be A Better READER

STARTING OUT

GLOBE FEARON
Pearson Learning Group

Reviewers

Kathleen F. Crocco
Special Education Teacher
Barrett Middle School
Columbus, OH

Victoria Goon
Instructional Support Teacher–Reading
McEvoy Middle School
Macon, GA

Lynn McPeak
Assistant Superintendent
Empire Union School District
Modesto, CA

Dr. Darlene Ponder
Instructional Specialist
Dallas Public Schools
Dallas, TX

Jean Wennell
Program Director
New Hope Charter School
Lodi, CA

Art and Design: Tricia Battipede, Robert Dobaczewski, Elizabeth Witmer
Editorial: Brian Hawkes, Eleanor Ripp, Jennifer M. Watts
Manufacturing: Michele Uhl
Production: Laura Benford-Sullivan, Jeffrey Engel
Publishing Operations: Jennifer Van Der Heide

Copyright © 2003 by Pearson Education, Inc., publishing as Globe Fearon, an imprint of Pearson Learning Group, 299 Jefferson Road, Parsippany, NJ 07054. All rights reserved. No part of this book may be reproduced or transmitted in any form or by any means, electronic, or mechanical, including photocopying, recording, or by any information storage and retrieval system, without permission in writing from the publisher. For information regarding permission(s), write to Rights and Permissions Department.

Printed in the United States of America
5 6 7 8 9 10   06 05

ISBN 0-130-23923-2

Photo Credits:

All photos © Pearson Learning unless otherwise noted.
Cover: Background: © Robert Karpa/Masterfile. l.: Per-Eric Berglund/The Image Bank. m.l.: Steve Cole/PhotoDisc, Inc. m.r.: Jeffrey Coolidge/The Image Bank. r.: Coneyl Jay/Stone.
Page Header: Per-Eric Berglund/The Image Bank.
p. 14 Bettmann/CORBIS; **p. 19** AP/Wide World; **p. 23** Stone; **p. 38** AP Photo/Mark Foley; **p. 39** David Young-Wolff, PhotoEdit; **p. 43** AP Photo/Serge Ligtenberg; **p. 44** Corbis Digital Stock; **p. 62** Corbis; **p. 68** PhotoDisc, Inc.; **p. 69** PhotoDisc, Inc; **p. 88** Odyssey Production; **p. 89** Stone; **p. 111** Hulton Getty/Liaison Agency, Inc.; **p. 117** Stone; **p. 117** Animals Animals/Earth Scenes; **p. 118** Stone; **p. 118** Tom McHugh, Photo Researchers

1-800-321-3106
www.pearsonlearning.com

Contents

UNIT 1 FROM HERE TO THERE 6

1. Character 6
   LITERATURE SELECTION "Thin Ice"
2. Main Idea and Details 11
   SOCIAL STUDIES SELECTION "Marco Polo's Travels"
3. Drawing Conclusions 17
   SCIENCE SELECTION "Hurricanes"
4. Word Problems 22
   MATHEMATICS SELECTION "Solving Word Problems"
5. Consonant Sounds 25
6. Long and Short Vowel Sounds 26
7. Plural Nouns 27
8. Reading a Map 28
9. Using a Recipe 29

UNIT 2 PROBLEMS AND SOLUTIONS 30

10. Plot 30
    LITERATURE SELECTION "The Man With the Cane"
11. Steps in a Process 35
    SOCIAL STUDIES SELECTION "The Recycling Solution"
12. Comparing and Contrasting 41
    SCIENCE SELECTION "Power for the Future"
13. Reading Percents 46
    MATHEMATICS SELECTION "Understanding Percents"
14. Consonant Blends 49
15. Long Vowel Sounds 50
16. Contractions 51
17. Multiple-Meaning Words 52
18. Reading a Graph 53
19. Using a Bus Schedule 54

UNIT 3 TIME FOR COURAGE 55

20. Setting 55
    LITERATURE SELECTION "Stop the Train"
21. Fact and Opinion 60
    SOCIAL STUDIES SELECTION "The Code Talkers"

22.	Cause and Effect SCIENCE SELECTION "The Space Shuttle"	65
23.	Reading Metric Terms MATHEMATICS SELECTION "Going Metric"	71
24.	*r*-Controlled Vowel Sounds	74
25.	Silent Letters	75
26.	Possessive Nouns	76
27.	Prefixes and Suffixes	77
28.	Reading a Table	78
29.	Using the Yellow Pages	79

UNIT 4 PAST AND PRESENT — 80

30.	Theme LITERATURE SELECTION "Obu and the Sea Princess"	80
31.	Cause and Effect SOCIAL STUDIES SELECTION "Ruling the Inca Empire"	85
32.	Making Generalizations SCIENCE SELECTION "The Greenhouse Effect"	91
33.	Word Problems MATHEMATICS SELECTION "Solving Word Problems That Have Too Much Information"	96
34.	Hard and Soft *c* and *g*	99
35.	Compound Words	100
36.	Using Parts of a Book	101
37.	Reading a Diagram	102
38.	Reading Classified Ads	103

UNIT 5 OTHER WORLDS — 104

39.	Conflict and Resolution LITERATURE SELECTION "Greetings!"	104
40.	Main Idea and Details SOCIAL STUDIES SELECTION "The Mystery of Stonehenge"	109
41.	Sequence of Events SCIENCE SELECTION "Helping Endangered Animals Survive"	115
42.	Reading Mathematical Terms MATHEMATICS SELECTION "Points and Lines"	120
43.	Vowel Digraphs	123
44.	Diphthongs	124
45.	Syllables	125
46.	Reading a Dictionary Entry	126
47.	Reading a Food Label	127

To the Student

Welcome to *Be A Better Reader: Starting Out*. This book will help you master the skills that you need to better understand your textbooks, stories, and other types of everyday reading.

READING SELECTION LESSONS

Each unit in the book has four lessons with reading selections. These lessons include the following sections.

Word Attack Strategies Word Attack Strategies appear on the first page of each lesson. The page has three parts. In the first part, you will work with a phonics skill—the sounds that vowels and consonants make. In the second part, you will learn about the structure of words—prefixes, word endings, base words, and so on. The third section is called Word Clues. It helps you figure out the meaning of new words by using clues in nearby sentences.

Skill Focus The second page of each lesson teaches an important reading skill, such as identifying the main idea or drawing conclusions. Practicing these skills will help you understand and remember what you read.

Reading Selections Each lesson includes a reading selection. The first lesson in each unit has a literature selection, which is a short story. The second lesson has a social studies selection. The third has a science selection. Finally, each unit includes a mathematics selection. The selections will help you acquire skill in reading in these four areas.

Comprehension At the end of each lesson is a page of activities. Comprehension is the first of these activities. The answers to comprehension questions can be found in the selection. You may need to reread part of a selection to find these answers.

Critical Thinking The second activity asks questions whose answers are not stated directly in the selection. To answer these questions, you will need to use information in the text and what you already know.

Skill Focus The last activity asks you to use the skill that you learned in the Skill Focus section on the lesson's second page. If you have a problem answering any of these questions, you can reread the Skill Focus.

Reading-Writing Connection Each lesson ends with a Reading-Writing Connection. This is a chance to write your own ideas and feelings about each selection.

SKILLS LESSONS

Each unit also includes several one-page skills lessons. Some of these lessons review the Word Attack Strategies you learned in the reading selection lessons. Other lessons help you understand maps, graphs, charts, schedules, ads, food labels, and other real-world reading.

The skills you learn in this book will help you become a better reader. Look for chances to use these skills in school and at home. The more you practice, the more your reading will improve!

UNIT 1 — FROM HERE TO THERE

Lesson 1 Character

Reading a Literature Selection

When is it a good idea to take a chance? When is it better to choose a safer course? In "Thin Ice," you will read about a character who takes a chance.

WORD ATTACK STRATEGIES

■ Initial and Final Consonants

When you are reading, it is important to look at the **consonants** at the beginning and the end of words. Look at the words in the box. You will see them again in the story.

scream	cold	bigger	water
heat	crack	safe	middle

1. Write the word from the box that begins with the same consonant as the words on each line.

bikes better _bigger_

month mountain _____

2. Write the word from the box that ends with the same consonant as the words on each line.

without went _heat_

arm problem _scream_

■ Verb Endings

The ending *-ed* can be added to most verbs to show an action in the past. Some verbs change spelling when adding *-ed*. Verbs that end with a vowel followed by a consonant double the consonant before adding *-ed*.

slam	slammed

When you see *-ed* at the end of a word, decide if the word is a verb. If it is, look for the base form of the verb. Read the sentence below. Think about the word in dark type.

Jed **grabbed** his friend's arm.

You may not know the word *grabbed*. If you know the word *grab*, however, you can figure out what *grabbed* means.

3. Find the verb with the *-ed* ending in the sentence below. Write its base form.

Jed gripped the ice with his feet. _grip_

■ Word Clues

As you read the story, you will see some new words. Look for clues to their meaning in nearby sentences. Read the sentences below. What clues help you figure out the meaning of the underlined word?

Matt's body was <u>shivering</u> with cold. He couldn't stop shaking.

You may not know what *shivering* means. The words *with cold* and *shaking* are clues. *Shivering* means "shaking with cold."

4. As you read "Thin Ice," use word clues to figure out the underlined words. Draw a line from each word to its correct meaning.

bank —————— carefully
cautiously ⨯ land near a river
dragged —————— pulled

SKILL FOCUS

■ **Character**

How can you tell if someone is friendly or not friendly? How do you know if a person is fair or mean? Usually, you can tell what a person is like by watching what that person does or says. You can also learn about people from what others say about them.

You learn about story characters in the same ways. **Characters** are the people in a story. Story characters say and do things that show what they are like. A writer might show you a character's thoughts, too.

Read these paragraphs from the story "Thin Ice." Use details from the paragraphs to figure out what the character Matt is like.

> Jed and Matt were walking home from school. It was the first really cold day of winter. "The ice on the river is hard!" Matt shouted. "Let's take a shortcut across."
>
> Jed made a face. "It just started to freeze," said Jed. "I don't think it's safe."
>
> "You're afraid of everything," said Matt with a laugh. "If you want to walk all the way to the bridge, go ahead. I'm going to cross here." Then he raced toward the river.
>
> Jed stood still, thinking. Why was Matt always doing things he wasn't supposed to? He seemed to like getting into trouble. Jed was different. If there was one thing Jed didn't like, it was trouble.

You could use a Character Map like this to show what Matt is like.

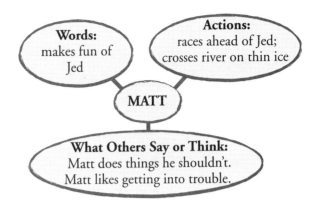

5. Read all the details about Matt on the map. Then write one or two sentences that describe what kind of person he is.

He was thoughtless and he liked danger.

■ **Strategy Tip** ■

Look for details that show what the characters in a story are like. Look for details about what the characters say and do. Also look for their thoughts and what others say or think about them.

Lesson 1 Character 7

Thin Ice

Words to Know

shortcut (SHORT kuht)
a shorter, more direct way to get somewhere

afraid (ə FRAYD)
feeling fear

dangerous (DAYN jər əs)
not safe

hero (HIR oh)
someone who does something important to help others

Jed and Matt were walking home from school. It was the first really cold day of winter. "The ice on the river is hard!" Matt shouted. "Let's take a **shortcut** across."

Jed made a face. "It just started to freeze," said Jed. "I don't think it's safe."

"You're **afraid** of everything," said Matt with a laugh. "If you want to walk all the way to the bridge, go ahead. I'm going to cross here." Then he raced toward the river.

Jed stood still, thinking. Why was Matt always doing things he wasn't supposed to do? He seemed to like getting into trouble. Jed was different. If there was one thing Jed didn't like, it was trouble.

Matt had reached the river and was about to step onto the ice. "I'll go look at the ice," Jed said. "Maybe it is strong enough."

When Jed got to the river, Matt was already out on the ice. Jed saw right away that the ice was too thin. It looked **dangerous**. He could see the river water moving under the ice.

"You'd better come back," Jed called to Matt. "The water is deep under that ice!"

Matt didn't listen. By now, he was near the middle of the river. "Are you still afraid, Jed?" he laughed. "Look how thick the ice is." Matt jumped up and down a few times to prove his point.

Crack! A loud sound filled the air. Matt looked down. In all directions, the thin ice was breaking away from his feet. Another crack, and Matt was in the river!

Matt went down like a rock. The cold water hurt. Up above him, he saw light and the cracks in the ice. He grabbed for the ice. "Help!" Matt screamed. His wet clothes pulled him down.

Safe on the dry land of the bank of the river, Jed looked around. There was no one else to help. If he ran to get help, Matt would go under. If he went out on the ice, it might break under him. What should Jed do?

Cautiously, Jed felt the ice, carefully testing the area around him. Using his feet, he pushed himself slowly toward the hole in the ice. Matt waved his arms and began to scream again. "Keep still," Jed ordered, "or we'll both go under!"

Jed took Matt's arm. He tried to pull him out of the water. But Matt was bigger than Jed. Jed could feel himself heading toward the water. He had to let go of Matt. Screaming, Matt fell back under.

Somehow, Matt got his head up out of the water again. Jed was still there. Again he took hold of Matt's hand. Jed gripped the ice with his feet. He pulled and pulled. Little by little, he dragged Matt out of the water.

The danger was not over, however. The ice gave another crack. It could give way at any time, and Matt was freezing in the cold.

Slowly, Jed dragged Matt across the ice. After what seemed like hours, they reached the land. Matt's body was shivering with cold. He couldn't stop shaking.

"Do something, Jed," Matt cried. "I'm freezing!"

Jed looked around. Route 67 wasn't far away. "That way!" he ordered.

The first car to pass was a police car. Jed waved his arms. He jumped up and down to make the car stop. It was Officer Crane.

Officer Crane helped Matt into the car. She gave him a blanket. She turned up the heat in the car. After hearing the story, Officer Crane said, "Well, Jed, it sounds like you are a **hero**. Maybe I should call the newspaper. Someone from the paper can come down and take your picture and write an article."

"Good idea," said Matt. He was feeling a lot better. "I have never had my picture in the paper."

"I was talking about *Jed's* picture," said Officer Crane. "He's the hero."

Jed thought for a minute. "No, you'd better not," he said. "My mom told me to stay away from the river. If she finds out, she will ground me for sure. I won't be able to go anywhere for weeks."

However, Jed couldn't keep the story a secret. Somehow, the newspaper found out. There was an article called "Hero Saves Friend in River," along with Jed's picture.

Jed's mom didn't ground him, but Matt's mom grounded her son. Matt didn't really mind. After being in the river, just being home felt good!

| **Comprehension** | Write the answers to the following questions on the lines. |

1. Why didn't Jed want Matt to go onto the ice? He didn't want him to go to the ice because was not safe.
2. After Jed pulled Matt out of the river, what problems did the boys still face? The danger was not over stop. Matt was shivering and cold.
3. Why didn't Jed want the newspaper to write this story? Jed didn't want the newspaper to write about the story because he was afraid of his mom.

| **Critical Thinking** | Write the answers to the following questions. You will have to figure out the answers because they are not directly stated in the selection. |

4. When he first tried to pull Matt out, why did Jed suddenly let go of Matt's hand? He thought they'd both go under. He wanted to himelf.
5. Do you think Jed did the right thing when he went out on the ice to save Matt? Why? Yes. because no body can help him in the ice.

| **Skill Focus** | In the circles, write details about Jed that show what kind of person he is. Then write a sentence that describes Jed's character. |

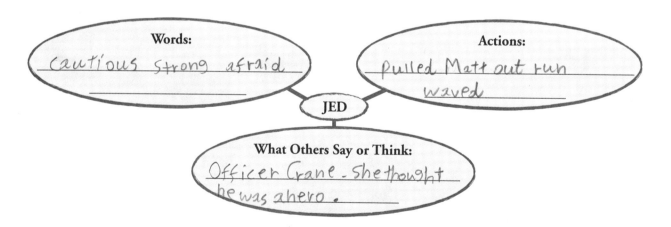

Words: cautious strong afraid

Actions: pulled Matt out run waved

JED

What Others Say or Think: Officer Crane - She thought he was a hero.

6. Sentence Describing Jed: Jed is a god frind and a Hero.

| **Reading-Writing Connection** | Suppose you are the reporter who wrote about Jed. On another sheet of paper, write a paragraph from the newspaper article. |

Lesson 2 Main Idea and Details

Reading a Social Studies Selection

This selection tells the true story of an explorer named Marco Polo. He was one of the first people from Europe to visit China more than 700 years ago.

WORD ATTACK STRATEGIES

■ Short Vowel Sounds

Many words have **short vowel sounds**. You hear the short *a* sound at the beginning of *at*. Other short vowel sounds are *e* as in *egg*, *i* as in *it*, *o* as in *on*, and *u* as in *but*. When a word has only one vowel and when that vowel is not at the end of the word, the vowel usually has a short vowel sound.

The words below have short vowel sounds.

land   went   ships   spot   uncle

1. Circle the words with short vowel sounds.

home   (job)   take   (rich)   (facts)
(trip)   (up)   (left)   leave   cake

■ The *-er* Ending

The ending *-er* can be added to many words. It means "one who." A *ruler*, for example, is "one who rules." Look at the words below that end in *-er*.

ruler   listener   prisoner

Read the sentence below. Think about the word in dark type.

He was a good **listener** and remembered everything.

You may not know the word *listener*. If you know *listen*, however, you can figure out that *listener* means "one who listens."

2. Circle the word that ends in *-er* in the sentences below. Write its meaning.

Marco Polo went to prison. He was a prisoner in Genoa.

prisoner: somone who is in the prison.

■ Word Clues

As you read about Marco Polo, you will see some new words. Try to figure out what they mean. Look for clues in nearby sentences. Read the sentence below. What clues help you figure out the underlined word?

The Silk Road went through a great <u>desert</u>. There was hardly any water.

You may not know what *desert* means. The next sentence, however, helps you guess. A *desert* is "a place with hardly any water."

3. As you read "Marco Polo's Travels," you will see some underlined words. Use word clues to figure out their meanings. Write the correct word in each blank below.

traveled   refused   <u>fabulous</u>

Marco Polo _traveled_ to China. He saw _fabulous_ things that people did not have in Europe. The ruler of China _refused_ to let Polo go home.

SKILL FOCUS

■ **Identifying Main Ideas and Details**

Suppose you wanted to draw a picture to show how much fun you have at the beach. You might show people swimming, playing volleyball, and listening to the radio. When people looked at these details, they would get the message: Going to the beach is fun.

The same thing happens in writing. Writers want to tell you about their **main ideas**. The main ideas are what their writing is about. To make sure you get these main ideas, writers give many **details**.

Often each paragraph in an article has one main idea. Sometimes one sentence gives the main idea. The other sentences give details that tell more about the main idea.

Read this paragraph from "Marco Polo's Travels." Look for the main idea and the details that tell more about it.

> Traveling on the Silk Road was not easy or safe. It went through a great desert. There was hardly any water. The Silk Road also went over high mountains. Travelers were often attacked along the way.

The first sentence gives the main idea. The other sentences give details. You could use a Main Idea and Details Map to show the main idea and details.

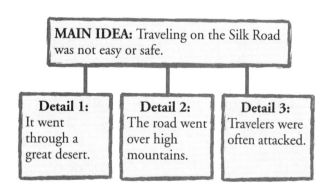

4. Read the following paragraph from the selection. Underline the main idea. Then, find four details that tell more about the main idea. Write them on the lines.

> <u>China was far ahead of Europe</u> at this time. The Chinese, for example, used paper money. Polo had never seen that. They also burned "black rocks" for heat. These rocks were coal. Letters moved quickly from place to place. Books were printed by machine, not written by hand. Young Marco Polo could not believe all he saw.

Detail 1: _The Chinese used paper money._

Detail 2: _Burned black rocks._

Detail 3: _Letters moved quickly from place to place by that time._

Detail 4: _Young Marco polo could not belive all he saw._

■ **Strategy Tip** ■

As you read the selection, think about the main idea of each paragraph. Then look for the details that tell more about the main idea.

Marco Polo's Travels

Words to Know

trade (trayd)
to buy and sell goods

voyage (VOI əj)
to make a trip by ship

Silk Road (silk rohd)
a very long road that ran from Europe to China; it was first used more than 2,000 years ago

court (kort)
the place where a ruler and his or her helpers live and work

The Trip to China

Marco Polo was born in Venice (VEN əs), Italy, in the year 1254. When he was 17, he left home to go to China. He had no idea that his trip would take 24 years.

On his trip, Polo traveled with his father and his uncle. The Polos hoped to trade with the Chinese. Things made in China were worth a lot of money in Europe then.

The Polos wanted to go to China by ship. However, they could not find any ships that were strong enough to make the long voyage. So they had to go over land. The Silk Road across Asia was the only way. Traveling

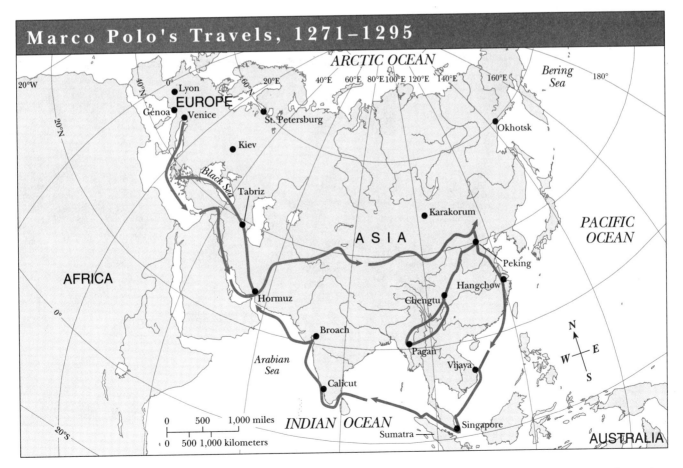

Marco Polo's Travels, 1271–1295

Lesson 2 Main Idea and Details 13

on the Silk Road was not easy or safe. It went through a great desert. There was hardly any water. The Silk Road also went over high mountains. Travelers were often attacked along the way. After three long years, the Polos reached China. At that time, a man named Kublai Khan (KOO blə kahn) was the ruler of China. The Polos went to visit his **court**. Right away, Kublai Khan liked Marco Polo.

Working for Kublai Khan

Kublai Khan gave Polo an important job. Polo had to travel all over China for the ruler. He told the people what their ruler wanted. He also had to bring back information about what was happening across China.

China was far ahead of Europe at this time. The Chinese, for example, used paper money. Polo had never seen that. They also burned "black rocks" for heat. These rocks were coal. Letters moved quickly from place to place. Books were printed by machine, not written by hand. Young Marco Polo could not believe all he saw.

Marco Polo traveled all over Asia. He went into Tibet (tə BET) and Burma (BER mə). He also heard stories about a rich land to the east. Today, we call this land Japan.

Marco Polo wrote down things that he saw. He was able to send many facts to Kublai Khan. Polo also liked to talk with poor people and farmers. He was a good listener and remembered everything. Kublai Khan liked hearing about these things.

The Voyage Home

After many years, Marco Polo wanted to leave China. He was almost 40 years old. He had worked for Kublai Khan for 17 years. Polo missed his home in Venice. He missed his family and friends there. Polo's father and uncle wanted to go home, too. By that time, they were rich from all their trades.

Kublai Khan **refused** to let Marco Polo leave China. He liked Polo too much. He also needed his help. Polo asked to leave many times, but Kublai Khan always said no.

This painting shows Kublai Khan welcoming the Polos in his court.

In the year 1292, Marco Polo got a chance to go home. A princess from Kublai Khan's court was going to Persia (PER zhə). She was going to marry a king there. Kublai Khan said Polo could go on the trip. His job was to keep the princess safe. After the trip, Polo was supposed to come back.

In all, 14 ships and more than 600 people made the trip. First, they went south to a place we now call Singapore (SING ə por). Then they traveled around Sumatra (soo MAH trə) and the tip of India.

The ships were attacked many times along the way. Hundreds of men were killed in the fighting. The Polos and the princess, however, were not hurt. At last, they crossed the Arabian (ə RAY bee ən) Sea and landed in Persia.

Kublai Khan had ordered Marco Polo to come back to China. Polo, however, had other ideas. After leaving the princess in Persia, the Polos went north to the Black Sea. From there, they took ships to Venice. Marco Polo never saw China—or Kublai Khan—again.

Coming Home and Going to War

Marco Polo got home in the year 1295. He had been gone 24 years. He had traveled 15,000 miles. His travels in China had made him a rich man.

Polo's story does not end there, however. In the year 1296, Venice went to war with Genoa (JEN oh ə), another Italian city. Polo wanted to fight for Venice. He became the leader of a fighting ship.

Venice lost the war. Marco Polo and his men were put in prison in Genoa. Polo was a prisoner for more than a year.

Marco Polo Tells His Story

To pass the time, Polo told stories about his years in China. The other prisoners liked hearing about his adventures. They loved listening to tales of the many wonders Polo talked about. Few people in Europe had heard about China in those days. Many of Marco Polo's stories seemed unbelievable. They sounded too fabulous to be true.

One day, a prisoner named Rustichello (RUS tee kel oh) heard Polo talking. Rustichello had been a writer before the war. He asked if he could write a book about Polo's adventures. Polo said yes and told all the stories again from the beginning. Rustichello wrote them down as Polo talked.

The war ended, and Polo got out of prison. He went back to Venice and got married. He lived to be 70 years old.

An Important Book

Marco Polo's book came out in 1298. It was called *The Description of the World*. At this time, books had to be written by hand in Europe. Even so, many people read the book. Some readers thought Polo had made it all up.

Explorers, however, thought Polo's book was important. Christopher Columbus, for example, read the book almost 200 years later. It helped him see the world in a new way. It helped him plan for his voyage to the East.

Not too long after Polo left, Kublai Khan lost his power. China was closed to outsiders. No one from Europe went there again until the 1500s. People started to forget about Kublai Khan. Much information about him was lost.

Polo's book, however, lives on. People still read it today. It tells us about life in China more than 700 years ago.

| **Comprehension** | Write the answers to the following questions on the lines. |

1. Why did Marco Polo take the Silk Road to China? _He took the Silk Road to China because was the only way by land_

2. What job did Marco Polo have in China? _He had to travel all ove China for the ruler. He told the people what their ruler wanted and he also had to bring back information about what was hapening across China._

3. What important things happened to Polo after his return from China? _He wanted to fight for Venice. Venice lost the war. Marco and his men were put in the prisoner. He got married._

| **Critical Thinking** | Write the answers to the following questions. You will have to figure out the answers because they are not directly stated in the article. |

4. Was it a good idea for Kublai Khan to ask an outsider to bring him information? Why or why not? _Yes it was a good idea because he told the people what their ruler wanted._

5. Why did some people not believe the stories in Polo's book at first? _Some people didn't believe his stories because they thought he had made them up._

| **Skill Focus** | Circle the main idea of each paragraph below. Then underline three details that tell more about the main idea. |

6. After many years, Marco Polo wanted to leave China. He was almost 40 years old. He had worked for Kublai Khan for 17 years. Polo missed his home in Venice. He missed his family and friends there. Polo's father and uncle wanted to go home, too. By that time, they were rich from all their trades.

7. Kublai Khan refused to let Marco Polo leave China. He liked Polo too much. He also needed his help. Polo asked to leave many times, but Kublai Khan always said no.

| **Reading-Writing Connection** | Why is it still important for people to learn about life in other lands? On another sheet of paper, write a paragraph telling what you think. |

Lesson 3 Drawing Conclusions

Reading a Science Selection

Hurricanes are very strong storms that can break trees and smash houses. In this selection, you will find out how hurricanes form and how scientists study them.

WORD ATTACK STRATEGIES

■ **Long Vowel Sounds**

Many words have **long vowel sounds**. When a word contains just two vowels and one of the vowels is a final *e*, the first vowel is usually long. The final *e* is silent. For example, you can hear a long *a* sound in *lake*, a long *i* in *time*, a long *o* in *broke*, and a long *u* in *cute*.

The words in the box below have long vowel sounds.

| wave | space | rise | wide | those |

1. Circle the words that have a long vowel sound.

(race)   (fine)   trick   pat
spot   (white)   west   (home)

■ **Plural Endings**

A **singular** noun names one person, place, idea, or thing. A **plural** noun names more than one. Most nouns form their plurals by adding *-s*. Some nouns, however, add *-es*. Look at the plural nouns below.

| beaches | businesses | bushes | stories |

Nouns that end in *-s, -ss, -ch, -sh, -x,* or *-z* add the plural ending *-es*. Nouns that end in a consonant and *y*, such as *family*, also add the *-es* ending. First, though, you must change the *y* to *i*, as in *families*. Read the following sentence. Think about the word in dark type.

Hurricanes hit the **beaches** first.

You may not know the word *beaches*. If you know *beach*, though, you can figure out that *beaches* means "more than one beach."

2. Circle the plural noun in the sentence below. Write the singular form of the noun.

During the hurricane, one wave was three (stories) high. _Story_

■ **Word Clues**

As you read about hurricanes, you will see some new words. Look for clues to their meanings in nearby sentences. Sometimes, the writer gives you the meaning of a new word. Read the sentence below. What clues explain the underlined word?

The air over the sea also has to be moist, or filled with water.

You may not know what *moist* means. The rest of the sentence, however, tells you. *Moist* means "filled with water."

3. As you read "Hurricanes," use word clues to figure out the underlined words. Then, answer *yes* or *no* to the questions below.

Do the winds of a hurricane rotate? _Yes_

Do hurricanes damage buildings? _Yes_

Do neighborhoods become submerged during bad hurricanes? _Yes_

Lesson 3 Drawing Conclusions 17

SKILL FOCUS

■ Drawing Conclusions

Suppose you saw pictures of a town near the sea. In the pictures, trees are down. Houses are smashed. Some neighborhoods are under water. "What happened here?" you might ask. To answer your question, you could draw a conclusion.

A **conclusion** is a decision that is based on what you learn from reading or looking. Conclusions are also based on what you already know. For example, you might already know that powerful storms called hurricanes come in from the sea and destroy buildings. Using what you see in the pictures and what you already know, you can draw a conclusion: *A hurricane has hit the town.*

A writer cannot tell you everything in an article. Sometimes you will have to draw conclusions. As you read, think about the details. Make decisions about what they mean. Your conclusions should help you make sense of what you read.

Read the following sentences. What conclusion can you draw about the time or season when you might see a hurricane?

> Hurricanes hardly ever form in winter or spring. The waters of the sea must be warm—about 80°F—for a hurricane to form.

You already know that the air is warmest during the summer and early fall. The sea would be warm then, too. So you can conclude that most hurricanes form in summer and fall, when the sea is warm.

4. Read the following sentences. What conclusion can you draw about why hurricanes do more harm today? Write your conclusion on the lines below.

> More Americans today live near the sea than ever before. They build houses and businesses along the beach. Also, many people go to the beach during the summer and fall. So hurricanes do more harm than ever before.

Conclusion: <u>Hurricanes do more harm now than before because more people live near the sea than ever before. Also, more people go to the sea for vacation in the summer and fall.</u>

■ **Strategy Tip** ■

As you read the article about hurricanes, use what you learn and what you already know to draw conclusions. Drawing conclusions will help you get the most from your reading.

18 Lesson 3 Drawing Conclusions

Hurricanes

Words to Know

hurricanes (HER ə kaynz)
storms with winds of 75 miles per hour or faster

eye wall (eye wawl)
the part of a hurricane around the eye, or center; the eye wall has very strong winds

course (kors)
path

storm surge (storm serj)
a wall of seawater formed during a hurricane

Trees break in two. Houses are smashed. A wall of water leaves a neighborhood in ruins. The violence of **hurricanes** is hard to believe. What are these monster storms? How do they form?

How Do Hurricanes Begin?

Hurricanes begin over the sea. The sea has to be warm—about 80°F. The air over the sea also has to be moist, or filled with water.

In summer, warm, moist air rises off of the sea. This warm air moves up into the sky. At the same time, cool air moves in to take its place. This cool air begins to rotate, or move around in a circle. That moving air, or wind, is the beginning of the storm.

If the water stays warm, the storm grows. The winds rotate faster and faster. The winds are packed with seawater. The rotating air and rain look like a big, round wheel.

Sometimes the winds blow at 75 miles per hour or more. Then the storm is a hurricane. Many hurricane winds are even faster than that. The really harmful ones may have winds that blow at more than 155 miles per hour.

What Does a Hurricane Look Like?

Most hurricanes are about 300 miles wide.

This photograph of a hurricane is taken from the space shuttle. Computer details of lands, such as Florida and the islands, have been added.

They reach 40,000 feet into the sky. The power from one hurricane would make enough electricity to run the United States for six months!

People have taken pictures of hurricanes from space. A hurricane looks like a big, white wheel. At the center of the wheel is a calm spot called the eye. The whole hurricane rotates around the quiet eye.

A ring of storms is around the eye. Those storms form the **eye wall**. The winds in the eye wall are very strong. Over the sea, they kick up high waves. Some waves are three stories high.

The eye wall makes a loud screaming sound. If you were under the eye wall, you would not be able to hear anything else.

The eye of the storm, however, is calm. The sky is sunny. Birds caught inside the eye can ride out a hurricane. The eye is usually about 20 miles across.

The eye of a hurricane is not harmless, however. It can trick people into thinking that a hurricane is over. They come out of their homes. Then, suddenly, the wind and rain start again as the other side of the hurricane hits. The second part is as bad as the first.

When and Where Do Hurricanes Form?

In the Atlantic and Pacific oceans, most storms form between June and November. September is the top hurricane month. Many hurricanes begin as small storms in the Atlantic Ocean off Africa. Winds push the storms west. The storms move slowly at first, picking up power over the sea.

No two storms follow the same **course**. Some move in a straight line. Others jump around. A storm may hit islands in the Caribbean (kə RIB ee ən) Sea. It may then hit Florida or swing into the Gulf of Mexico. Some hurricanes hit land as far west as Texas or Mexico. Others race up the Atlantic coast to Georgia and the Carolinas.

What Happens When a Hurricane Hits?

When hurricanes hit, they can do a lot of damage, or harm. Hurricane winds smash into a neighborhood. Parts of buildings, bikes, and bushes fly through the air. People who are hit by these things can be killed.

Rain also does great damage during a hurricane. Many hurricanes can drop almost a foot of rain in a day. Some neighborhoods are submerged, or placed under water, after a bad hurricane.

The most harmful part of a hurricane is a crashing wall of water called the **storm surge**. Of every ten people who die in a hurricane, the storm surge kills nine.

The storm surge forms out at sea. The hurricane pushes down on the sea below it. The seawater is lower there. The eye of the hurricane, however, does not push down. The water below the eye is higher. This high water under the eye is the storm surge.

When a hurricane hits land, the storm surge is a wall of water. It can be 25 feet high and many miles wide. The surge crashes into buildings along the beaches.

Why Do Scientists Watch for Hurricanes?

Today, more Americans than ever before live near the oceans. They have built houses, apartments, and businesses there. Therefore, a bad hurricane does more damage today. In 1992, Hurricane Andrew caused more than $20 billion in damage.

No one can stop a hurricane from doing damage. However, scientists help people get through them. At the National Hurricane Center in Miami, Florida, scientists use computers to watch hurricanes form at sea. The scientists guess ahead of time the course of the storm. Often, they know 8 to 16 hours ahead of time where a storm will hit. People near the beaches then have time to leave for safer places. Hurricanes still ruin buildings, but people do not have to die in them.

Comprehension — Write the answers to the following questions on the lines.

1. What does a hurricane look like from space?
   A hurricane looks like a big white wheel.

2. How strongly do hurricane winds blow?
   The winds blow at 75 milles per hour or more.

3. What are three different ways that hurricanes do damage to towns?
   There ~~are~~ is damage, killed people and storm surge. rain/floods

Critical Thinking — Write the answers to the following questions. You will have to figure out the answers because they are not directly stated in the selection.

4. Why do people move away from the beach when they hear that a hurricane is coming?
   They move away from the beach so they can be safe and not get blow away.

5. Why is it hard to predict the course of a hurricane?
   It is hard to predict because it changes driection.

Skill Focus — Read the following paragraph. Then, draw a conclusion to answer the question below. Write your answer on the lines.

A hurricane hits Dana's town. Dana and her family are safe in their house. After an hour or so, the wind seems to stop. The rain does, too. The sky looks calm. Dana and her parents think about going out. They want to see how bad the damage is.

6. Why should Dana's family stay indoors, even though the hurricane seems to have passed?
   Because you don't know what it's going to happen next.

Reading-Writing Connection — Suppose a hurricane were about to hit your town. On another sheet of paper, tell what you would do to get ready for it.

Lesson 3 Drawing Conclusions 21

Lesson 4 Word Problems

Reading a Mathematics Selection

Can you think of some math problems you solve at home or at school? Many are probably word problems. In this selection, you will learn the five steps that will help you solve word problems.

WORD ATTACK STRATEGIES

■ Word Clues

As you read about solving word problems, you will see some new words. Look for clues to their meanings in nearby sentences.

Read the following sentence. What clues help you figure out the meaning of the underlined word?

guess ← <u>Estimate</u> the answer. When you estimate, you make a good guess.

You may not know the word *estimate*. In the next sentence, however, there is a clue to its meaning. *Estimate* means "make a good guess."

As you read "Solving Word Problems," use word clues to figure out the meanings of the underlined words. Then match each word with its meaning.

| decide | take away one number from another |
| subtract | figure out what to do |

SKILL FOCUS

■ Solving Word Problems

Tonya biked 11 miles on Saturday. On Sunday, she rode another 13 miles. <u>How far</u> did Tonya ride during the two days?

The paragraph above is a word problem. A **word problem** is a math problem that is written out in words rather than just in numbers. Think of a word problem as a puzzle. To solve this puzzle, you need to use reading and math skills at the same time.

Here are five steps you need to follow to solve word problems.

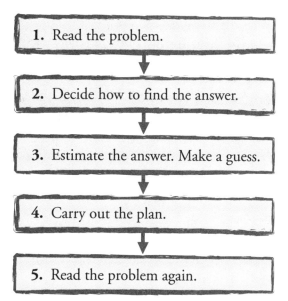

1. Read the problem.
2. Decide how to find the answer.
3. Estimate the answer. Make a guess.
4. Carry out the plan.
5. Read the problem again.

■ Strategy Tip ■

When you solve a word problem, use the five steps. Remember to follow them in the correct order. Work carefully through each step.

Solving Word Problems

Words to Know

round (round)
give in even units such as tens or hundreds

carry out (KAR ee out)
get done; bring to a finish

Monarch butterflies make a very long trip each year. During the trip, each <u>monarch</u> butterfly can lay hundreds of eggs. Some monarchs live only a few weeks. Some can live for as long as nine months.

Now that you know some facts about monarch butterflies, you can solve a word problem about them.

1. Read the problem.

One butterfly leaves from Canada and flies 1,940 miles to Mexico. Another butterfly leaves New York and flies 1,625 miles to Mexico. Which trip is shorter? How many miles shorter is it?

Are there any words that you do not know in the problem? If so, look them up in a dictionary. What does the problem ask? The last two sentences give the questions: *Which trip is shorter? How many miles shorter is it?*

2. Decide how to find the answer.

When you <u>decide</u>, or figure out, how to find the answer, it is sometimes helpful to make a drawing.

<u>1,940 miles</u>   trip from Canada

<u>1,625 miles</u>   trip from New York

Now look again at the problem. The question "Which trip is shorter?" indicates a comparison. To find how many miles shorter one trip is than another, you need to <u>subtract</u>, or take one number away from another.

3. Estimate the answer.

When you estimate, you make a good guess. **Round** the numbers to make an estimate. Round them to the nearest 100: 1,940 is about 1,900; 1,625 is about 1,600.

1,900 miles – 1,600 miles = 300 miles

Your estimate is 300 miles.

4. Carry out the plan.

When you **carry out** the plan, you do the math. Use the numbers from the problem. When you are finished, check your work.

1,940 miles – 1,625 miles = 315 miles

5. Read the problem again.

After reading the problem again, write the complete answer.

The trip from New York is 315 miles shorter.

Does the answer make sense? How close is the answer to your estimate? If the answer is not close, do the problem again.

You can use the five steps you just learned to help you solve all word problems.

| **Comprehension** | Write the answer to the following question on the lines. |

1. What are the five steps for solving word problems?
   Read the problem, Decide how to find the answer, Estimat the answer or make a guess, Carry out the plan, Read the problem again

| **Critical Thinking** | Write the answer to the following question. You will have to figure out the answer because it is not directly stated in the selection. |

2. Why is it important to make an estimate before you solve a word problem?
   An estimate helps you decide if you answer is correct.

| **Skill Focus** | Use the five steps to solve the following word problems. |

3. Read: One monarch butterfly lays 608 eggs. Another lays 594. How many eggs do they both lay?

Decide: +

Estimate: 608 + 594 = 1200
         600   600

Carry Out: 608 + 594 = 1202

Reread/Final Answer: The both lay 1202 eggs.

4. Read: One monarch butterfly lived 51 days. Another butterfly lived 274 days. How much longer did the second butterfly live? (Round the numbers to the nearest 10 to estimate.)

Decide: −

Estimate: 300

Carry Out:

Reread/Final Answer:

| **Reading-Writing Connection** | Look up more facts about monarch butterflies. Then write your own word problem. Trade papers with a partner. Solve the problems. |

24 Lesson 4 Word Problems

Lesson 5 Consonant Sounds

Look at each picture below. Say the name of the picture. Think about the **consonant sound** you hear at the beginning of each name. Then, write the letter that stands for that consonant sound.

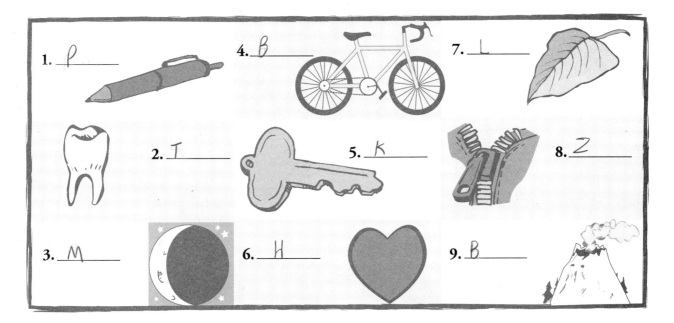

1. P
2. T
3. M
4. B
5. K
6. H
7. L
8. Z
9. B

Look at each picture below. Say its name. Listen to the ending sound. Write the letter that stands for the consonant sound you hear at the end of each name.

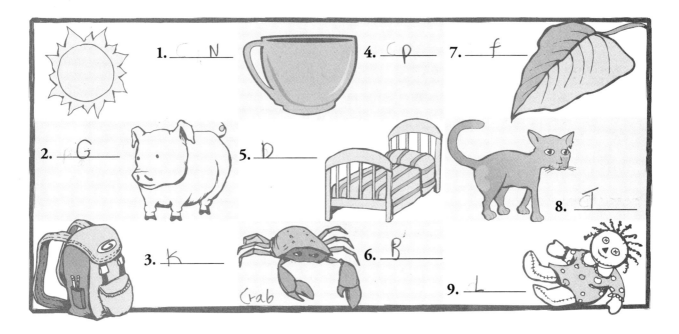

1. N
2. G
3. K
4. P
5. D
6. B
7. f
8. T
9. L

Lesson 5 Consonant Sounds 25

Lesson 6 Long and Short Vowel Sounds

Say the word *hat*. Listen for the *a* sound. The vowel *a* in *hat* has the short *a* sound. Next, say the word *hate*. Can you hear a different sound for *a*? The vowel *a* in *hate* has the long *a* sound.

Now say the name *Tim*. The vowel *i* in *Tim* has a **short vowel sound**. Now say the word *time*. The *i* in *time* has a **long vowel sound**.

Here are two rules to help you know when vowel sounds are short or long.

Rule 1: Many words have just one vowel. When the vowel is not at the end of the word, it usually has a short sound.

> hat   let   him   got   but

Rule 2: Many words contain two vowels, one of which is a final *e*. For most of these words, the first vowel is long and the final *e* is silent.

> make   scene   fine   close   use

Write *short* if the vowel sound is short. Write *long* if it is long.

1. dog __S__
2. home __L__
3. these __L__
4. ask __S__
5. less __S__
6. ate __L__
7. miss __S__
8. cut __S__
9. hot __S__
10. rode __L__
11. bike __L__
12. hit __S__
13. cute __L__
14. came __L__
15. fun __S__
16. eve __L__
17. sad __S__
18. line __L__
19. take __L__
20. sun __S__

Lesson 7   Plural Nouns

A **noun** names a person, place, thing, or idea. A **singular noun** names one person, place, thing, or idea. A **plural noun** names more than one person, place, thing, or idea. Most nouns change their endings when they become plurals.

Here are three rules for forming plural nouns.

Rule 1: Add the letter *-s* to form the plural of most nouns.

> ant—ant<u>s</u>   boy—boy<u>s</u>   store—store<u>s</u>

Rule 2: Add the letters *-es* to form the plural of nouns that end in *-s, -ss, -ch, -sh, -x,* or *-z.*

> dish—dish<u>es</u>   bus—bus<u>es</u>   class—class<u>es</u>   box—box<u>es</u>

Rule 3: If a noun ends in a consonant followed by the letter *y*, change the *y* to *i* and add the letters *-es* to form the plural.

> cry—cr<u>ies</u>   country—countr<u>ies</u>   family—famil<u>ies</u>

Write the plural of each noun below.

1. watch *watches*
2. story *stories*
3. worker *workers*
4. orange *oranges*
5. glass *glasses*
6. waltz *waltzes*
7. ending *endings*
8. business *businesses*
9. wish *wishes*
10. lunch *lunches*
11. change *changes*
12. fox *foxes*
13. boss *bosses*
14. body *bodies*
15. bush *bushes*
16. crash *crashes*
17. desk *desks*
18. study *studies*
19. ship *ships*
20. sickness *sicknesses*

Lesson 8 Reading a Map

In your social studies books, you will often see **maps**. Using a map will help you find all kinds of information about a place.

To use a map, first read the **title** of the map. The title tells you what the map shows. Also read the **caption**, the words under the map, to get more information about the map. Look at the **compass rose**, too. The compass rose shows the directions—north, south, east, and west. Also see if the map has a **key** or **legend**. The key lists the symbols used on the map and tells what they mean.

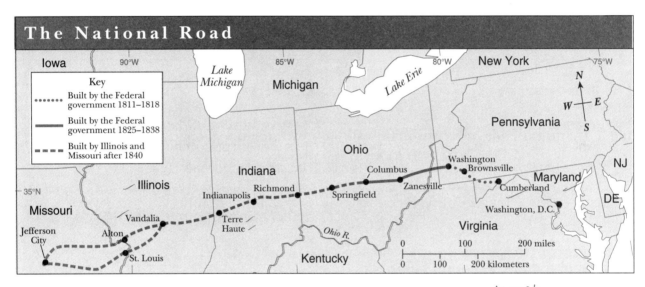

The National Road, also called the Cumberland Road, was the main road used to travel west from Maryland to Missouri in the 1800s.

Never
W weiners ———→ Eat
Sogy

Write the answers on the lines provided.

1. What is the title of the map? <u>The National Road.</u>

2. What cities in Ohio did the road pass through? <u>Springfield, Columbus and Zanesville.</u>

3. How does the key show you which part of the road was built between 1811 and 1818?
<u>........</u>

4. At what city did the National Road split into two roads? <u>Vandalia Illinois</u>

5. Which city on the National Road is closest to the border of Indiana and Illinois?
<u>Terre Haute</u>

6. At what city did the National Road start when it was first built? <u>Cumberland Maryland.</u>

Lesson 9 Using a Recipe

A **recipe** is a set of directions that tells how to prepare food. When you read a recipe, go through it quickly at first. Get an idea of what you have to do. Then read it again more carefully. Think about the order of the steps. For the recipe to work, you will have to follow the steps in the correct order.

Read the following recipe for "Grandma's Delights."

GRANDMA'S DELIGHTS

You will need:

2 egg whites	3/4 cup sugar
1/2 teaspoon vanilla	1-1/2 cups coconut flakes

Preheat the oven to 325°F. Separate the egg yolks from the whites. Place the egg whites in a bowl. Add vanilla to the egg whites. Beat until soft peaks form. Next, add the sugar slowly. Beat until the mixture is stiff. Then stir in the coconut. Drop rounded teaspoonfuls of the mixture onto a greased cookie sheet. Bake for 20 minutes.

Use the recipe to answer the questions below. Fill in the circle next to the best answer.

1. *After* adding the vanilla to the egg whites, the next step is to

    ○ separate the egg whites and yolks.

    ○ stir in the coconut.

    ◉ beat the mixture.

    ○ place the egg whites in a bowl.

2. What should you do *just before* dropping teaspoons of the mixture onto the cookie sheet?

    ◉ Preheat the oven.

    ○ Add the sugar slowly.

    ○ Stir in the coconut.

    ○ Beat the mixture until it is stiff.

3. Why is it important to follow the steps of a recipe in the correct order? _____

   <u>It's important to follow the steps of a recipe in the corrct order</u>
   <u>because</u>

UNIT 2 PROBLEMS AND SOLUTIONS

Lesson 10 Plot

Reading a Literature Selection

Do you like mysteries? Have you ever tried to solve one? The main character in this story finds herself in the middle of a mystery before she knows it!

WORD ATTACK STRATEGIES

■ **Consonant Blends**

Some words have two consonants at the beginning. If you can hear the sounds that both letters stand for, the letters are called a **blend**. The word *trash*, for example, begins with the blend *tr*. The word *clean* begins with the blend *cl*.

Look at the words in the box below. You will see them again in the selection.

| black | trick | broke |
| scooped | crowd | clear |

1. Say these words from the selection. Circle the blend that begins each word.

(st)uffed (bl)ue (pr)oblem
(cl)oset (sk)i (pl)ayed

■ **Contractions**

A **contraction** is a word that is the shortened form of two words. An apostrophe (') shows where one or more letters of the words have been left out.

Many contractions are formed from a pronoun and a verb. The pronoun *you* and the verb *will*, for example, can form the contraction *you'll*.

you + will = you'll

2. Match each pair of words with the contraction you can make from the words.

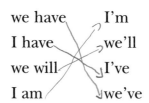

we have — I'm
I have — we'll
we will — I've
I am — we've

■ **Word Clues**

As you read the story, look for clues that help you figure out the meanings of new words. What clues help you figure out the meaning of the underlined word below?

The police had <u>arrested</u> the man with the strange eyes and were <u>holding</u> him in a cell at the police station.

If you don't know what *arrested* means, the words "holding him in a cell" are a clue. *Arrested* means "taken by the police and held for questioning about a crime."

3. As you read "The Man With the Cane," you will see some underlined words. Look for clues to their meanings. Then fill in the blanks below with the correct words.

confessed   identify   reward

At first, Sally and her father could not ___identify___ the robber. After the robber had ___confessed___ to the crime, Sally was offered a ___reward___.

SKILL FOCUS

■ **Understanding Plot**

Some stories really grab their readers' interest. They keep their readers' attention from start to finish. You have probably noticed that hard-to-put-down stories usually have great plots.

The **plot** is what happens in a story. The events, or happenings, in the story make up the plot. One event leads to the next in an interesting or exciting way.

Most plots center on a problem that a character faces. The events tell what the character does to solve his or her problem. The ending shows the solution to the problem.

You can use a Story Map to keep track of the plot of a story. The Story Map below shows the plot of "Thin Ice," the story you read on pages 8–9.

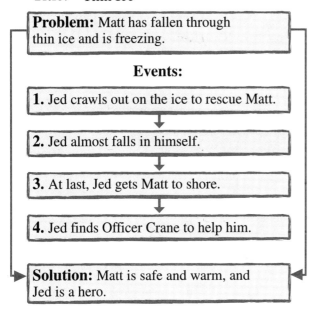

First, write the title of the story or movie. Then state the problem the main character faces. List four main events that happen. Finally, tell how the problem is solved.

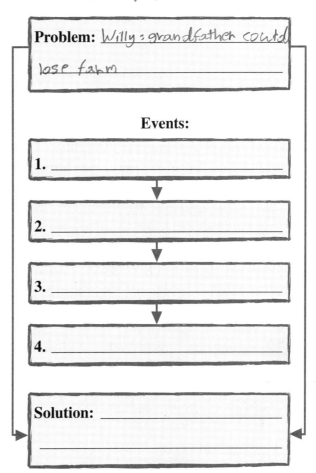

■ **Strategy Tip** ■

When you read a story, think about the problem that the main characters face. Keep track of what the characters do to solve their problem.

Now think about the plot of a story you have read or a movie you have seen recently. Use the following Story Map to show the plot.

Lesson 10 Plot 31

The Man With the Cane

Words to Know

criminal (CRIM ə nəl)
a person who commits a crime

evidence (EV ə dəns)
facts used to solve a case

witness (WIT nəs)
someone who sees a crime

disguise (dis GEYEZ)
items that hide who a person really is

Sally Robinson sat behind the counter of her father's store. She was counting the money the store had taken in that day. "Six hundred dollars, seven hundred . . ." Her father was in the back room.

Suddenly, a man in a red running suit and black ski mask burst through the door. Without a word, he walked to the counter. Once there, he scooped up the money and stuffed it into a bag.

"Dad!" Sally screamed, jumping off her stool.

Sally's father ran toward the counter as the man raced out of the door. Mr. Robinson pressed the alarm button. Then he and Sally hurried out onto the sidewalk.

The **criminal** was already half a block away. Soon Mr. Robinson, Sally, and a police car were all chasing the man.

Then a strange thing happened. The thief ran right into a white-haired man with a cane. The two fell in a tangled heap of legs and arms. The robber soon broke free and was running again.

"Are you okay?" Sally asked the white-haired man. She helped him to his feet. Handing him his cane, she couldn't help noticing his unusual eyes. One was green. The other was blue.

"Yes, yes, I'm fine," said the man, brushing himself off. "But I've got to leave. I'm already late." Then he hurried off.

Down the street, the police were getting closer to the robber. After a short chase, they caught him. Sally had to watch the store while her father went to the police station.

Mr. Robinson wasn't happy when he got back. "The robber didn't have any money on him when the police caught him!" Mr. Robinson moaned. "He didn't have the ski mask either. I couldn't identify his face because I never saw it. The police say they'll hold him for now, but the important evidence is gone! Worse yet, the other witness—the man with the cane—can't be found either!" Sally felt terrible. Losing $800 was a real problem. Somehow, she felt as if it were partly her fault. After all, she hadn't gotten the name of the man with the cane.

That night, Sally told her friend Maxine all about the robbery. When she was describing the man with the cane, Maxine interrupted her. "One blue eye and one green," Maxine said. "There's a man with eyes like that in apartment 13. He has just moved in." Maxine's father was in charge of making the repairs in their large apartment building.

"Does he use a cane and have white hair?" Sally asked.

"No, I don't think so," said Maxine.

"Well, he still might be the witness!" Sally said excitedly. "I want to talk to him."

The next day was Saturday. Sally was at Maxine's apartment early. When they went upstairs, no one was home in apartment 13. In the closet by the stairs, however, Sally saw something. In one corner, half covered with garbage bags, was a cane!

A strange idea suddenly flashed through Sally's mind. Maybe the man in apartment 13 didn't really need a cane. Maybe the cane was part of a **disguise**!

"Find something, girls?" a deep voice asked. Sally turned around slowly to look at the man who was talking to them. His hair wasn't white, but there was no mistaking those eyes!

"Hi," said Maxine. "We were just looking for you. My friend Sally wants to talk to you about a robbery."

The man was holding a clear plastic garbage bag. Inside, with the other garbage, were a white wig and a black ski mask.

"No, I don't want to talk!" Sally gasped. Grabbing Maxine's hand, she raced for the stairs. She could hear the man's footsteps just behind them.

"Hurry, Maxine!" Sally screamed. The girls ran down the stairs. The man was closer now. "If we can only make it to the street," thought Sally.

Bursting into the lobby, the girls slid across the marble floor and out of the open door. Sally was never so happy to see a Saturday morning crowd on Center Street. The man wouldn't try anything there.

Looking over her shoulder, Sally saw the man go back into the apartment building. "Hurry up, let's call 911!" Sally shouted.

"Fine! But will you *please* tell me what's going on?" Maxine demanded.

That afternoon, Detective Rodriguez came to the store to tell Sally and her father about the case. The police had arrested the man with the strange eyes and were holding him in a cell at the police station. The man was carrying $800 when he was arrested. Mr. Robinson would be getting the money back.

The man had confessed that the wig and the cane were a disguise. He had also admitted that he was a partner with the man in the running suit. The two men had planned the crime together. They had just pretended to have a collision so that the robber could give the money and the ski mask to the man with the cane. That way, if the runner was caught, there would be no evidence.

"And Sally," said Detective Rodriguez, as he left, "we'll call you about the reward."

"Reward?" said Sally, her eyes widening.

"Yes, you'll receive $5,000 for helping us catch these criminals," said the detective. "These men have played the same trick before. Now we've finally caught them!"

Comprehension	Write the answers to the following questions on the lines.

1. Who does the robber bump into after the robbery? Describe the second man in detail.
The robber bumped into a white-haired man with a cane.

2. Why is Sally so happy at the end of the story? Sally was so happy because the robber was caught and they got the money back.

Critical Thinking	Write the answers to the following questions. You will have to figure out the answers because they are not directly stated in the selection.

3. Why do you think the police couldn't find the man with the cane after the collision?
The police couldn't find the man, because he was wearing a disguise.

4. Why did Sally suddenly run away from the man in apartment 13? Sally suddenly ran away because she was afraid from him and wanted to call the police.

Skill Focus	Fill in the following Story Map. Show the plot for "The Man With the Cane."

Problem: Money was stolen from the store

Events:

1. The robber scooped up the money and stuffed it into a bag.

2. Sally and her father ran after the robber.

3. The police arrested the two men.

4. She got the money back.

Solution: The robber was caught.

Reading-Writing Connection	Does Sally deserve a reward for what she did? On another sheet of paper, write a paragraph that tells what you think.

Lesson 11 Steps in a Process

Reading a Social Studies Selection

Look around. Almost everything you see will be trash someday. In this selection, you'll find out how recycling can solve many of our trash problems.

WORD ATTACK STRATEGIES

■ Consonant Blends

In Lesson 10, you read about words that begin with consonant **blends** of two letters. Some words have three consonants at the beginning. If you can hear the sounds that each letter stands for, these three letters are also called a **blend**. The word *spread*, for example, begins with the blend *spr*. When you say *spread*, you can hear the sounds of the consonants *s*, *p*, and *r* blended together.

Look at the words in the box below. You will see them again in the selection.

| scraps *(left over)* | splinter *(sliver)* | strong |

1. Say each word below. Circle the consonant blend that begins each word.

(spr)ing   (str)eet   (scr)een

■ Contractions

A **contraction** is a shortened form of two words. An apostrophe (') shows where a letter or several letters have been left out. Many contractions are shortened forms of a verb and the word *not*. The verb *can* and the word *not*, for example, can be shortened to form the contraction *can't*.

can + not = can't

2. Write the two words from which each contraction was formed.

doesn't _does not_
don't _do not_
aren't _are not_

■ Word Clues

As you read, you will see some new words. Try to figure out what they mean. Details in nearby sentences will help you.

Read the following sentences. What clues help you figure out the underlined word?

> The best sites for landfills are low areas. However, low areas often fill up with rainwater in the spring. Plants grow there and feed many animals. Filling in these <u>wetlands</u> → *low areas fill up with rain water* with trash hurts the plants and animals.

You may not know what the word *wetlands* means. The nearby sentences, however, can help you guess. *Wetlands* are "low areas that often fill up with rainwater in the spring."

3. As you read "The Recycling Solution," look for the meanings of the underlined words. Match each word with its meaning.

shred — threads
fibers — cut up into little pieces
mulch — ground-up plant scraps spread around growing plants

SKILL FOCUS

■ Steps in a Process

How do you buy food from a snack machine? First, you drop the correct coins into the slot. Next, you press the correct button to choose your snack. Finally, you take your snack out of the machine.

Buying food from a snack machine is a **process**, a series of steps that must be done in order. Writers often describe a process. They give you the order of **steps in a process** from first to last. Sometimes clue words such as *first, second, next, then,* and *finally* help show the order.

Read the following paragraph from "The Recycling Solution." Follow the steps of the process shown in the Sequence Chart below.

> At the factory, the plastic bottles are first sorted. Next, they are ground up into chips. The chips are then washed and dried. The clean chips are poured into a large machine. Finally, long boards of "plastic wood" come out the other end of the machine.

Step 1: Plastic bottles are first sorted.

↓

Step 2: They are ground up into chips.

↓

Step 3: The chips are then washed and dried.

↓

Step 4: The clean chips are poured into a large machine.

↓

Step 5: Long boards of "plastic wood" come out the other end of the machine.

4. Read the following sentences from the selection. Follow the steps of the process. Write the steps in order on the chart below.

The farmers first shred, or cut up, the phone books into small pieces. Next, they put the shredded paper on their barn floors to soak up water and keep the floors dry. Later, they load the soiled paper into a spreader. Finally, farmers spread the shredded paper across the fields.

Step 1: cut up the phone books into small pieces.

↓

Step 2: Farmers put the shredded paper on the barn floors.

↓

Step 3: Later, they load the soiled paper into a spreader.

↓

Step 4: Farmers spread the shredded paper across the fields.

■ **Strategy Tip** ■

As you read the selection, pay attention to the processes the writer explains. Try to follow the steps of each process. Look for clue words such as *first, next,* and *then.*

The Recycling Solution

Words to Know

landfill (LAND fil)
place where trash is buried

incinerators (in SIN ə RAY tərz)
large furnaces for burning trash

recycling (ree SEYE kling)
using something over again

biodegradable (BEYE oh də GRAYD ə bəl)
able to break down in the ground

If you're like most Americans, you'll make four pounds of trash today. Only one pound will be recycled. The rest will be thrown away. It is likely to end up in a **landfill**.

The following graph shows what is thrown away in U.S. landfills. Notice that plastic and paper make up more than half of the garbage.

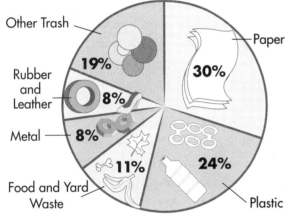

What Is Now in U.S. Landfills

- Other Trash 19%
- Rubber and Leather 8%
- Metal 8%
- Food and Yard Waste 11%
- Plastic 24%
- Paper 30%

The Landfill Problem

Right now, Americans have a landfill problem. Landfills are running out of room. In ten years, half the states will fill up their landfills.

Finding new landfills isn't easy. People don't want landfills in their towns. Besides, the best sites for landfills are low areas. However, low areas often fill up with rainwater in the spring. Plants grow there and feed many animals. Filling in these wetlands with trash will hurt the plants and animals.

Some towns burn trash in **incinerators**. The big furnaces do get rid of trash. However, dangerous smoke and ash are left behind. These hurt plants, animals, and people. Of course, most people don't want an incinerator on their street either.

The Recycling Solution

The best solution to the landfill problem is recycling. **Recycling** means using things again to cut waste. Recycling is becoming more common in the United States. However, not enough trash is recycled. For example, Americans recycle only 4 percent of their plastic. They throw away half of the paper they use, too.

Some Americans are now finding new ways to recycle. They are saving money and resources. Let's look at some new ways to recycle.

Plastic Wood, Plastic Cars

It is important to recycle plastic. That's because most plastic is not **biodegradable**. It doesn't rot or rust away as paper, yard waste, and metal do. Once plastic is in a landfill, it stays there for thousands of years.

People in Chicago are turning old plastic into playgrounds. Each week, they collect truckloads of empty plastic bottles. The bottles are sent to a nearby factory.

At the factory, the plastic bottles are first sorted. Next, they are ground up into chips. The chips are then washed and dried. The clean chips are poured into a large machine. Finally, long boards of "plastic wood" come out the other end of the machine.

The company ships the plastic wood back to Chicago. City workers there use the boards to rebuild playgrounds. About 350,000 plastic bottles make enough plastic wood for one playground. So far, hundreds of playgrounds have been rebuilt.

Park workers like the plastic wood. It doesn't rot or splinter. It doesn't stain either. Plastic wood can be sawed and bolted, just like real wood. By using plastic wood, Americans have already saved many forests.

These children are playing on a slide made of recycled plastic.

Could plastic replace the metal in cars? One car company thinks so. It recently made a car from milk jugs. The plastic car is strong enough to keep people safe. Yet it's also light in weight, so it uses less gas. A plastic car will never rust, so it doesn't even need to be painted.

People also recycle plastic into carpets, shoes, and clothing. However, they need to keep thinking of still more ways to recycle the plastic they use.

New Uses for Old Paper

Americans recycle almost half of their newspapers. They still throw away a lot of paper, though. Paper makes up about 30 percent of the trash in landfills. Finding new ways to recycle it is important.

Every year, for example, people throw away tons of old phone books. They should be recycling them instead. Dairy farmers have already found one new use for recycled phone books.

The farmers first shred, or cut up, the phone books into small pieces. Next, they put the shredded paper on their barn floors to soak up water and keep the floors dry. Later, they load the soiled paper into a spreader. Finally, farmers spread the shredded paper across their fields. The paper from the cow barns has rich food for the soil. Old phone books are now helping farmers.

The U.S. Postal Service recycles paper, too. Each year it has tons of junk mail it can't deliver. It can't return the mail either.

So the postal service started a pencil business. First, workers grind up the junk mail. Then they mix the paper powder with chemicals. Finally, the mixture is poured into molds to make pencils.

Postal workers use the pencils. They also give them to students. The pencils spread the news about recycling.

Phone books and junk mail are just a small part of the paper people waste. Still, every little bit helps. People everywhere have to find better ways to save and reuse paper.

Old Tires Bounce Back

Most of the rubber in landfills is made up of old tires. Americans throw away 265 million tires every year. Some of the tires are recycled. They come back as rubber floor mats and shoes. Other tires are burned to make electricity. Most of the tires end up in landfills, though.

Tires are hard to recycle because they contain more than just rubber. Most tires have steel in them, too. They also have plastic threads, or <u>fibers</u>. Workers must separate these materials for recycling.

New machines are doing just that. First, the machines chop the tires into pieces. Next, the small pieces are frozen and ground up. Big magnets then take out the steel. Finally, the machines press the rubber and plastic fibers through the holes of a metal screen. That forces the rubber away from the plastic.

Tire companies then use the rubber for new tires. Other companies spin the plastic fibers into cloth. The steel is used to make brand-new steel.

Trash Into Treasure

Food and yard wastes make up 11 percent of the trash in landfills. Nationwide, that is billions of tons. We could easily put this waste to use. In Florida, for example, one sixth-grade class runs a worm farm. The students feed the worms leftover food scraps from the lunchroom. It's a clean, modern process.

So far, the school has saved thousands of dollars. That's because it used to pay someone to dump the food waste. Now the worms turn the food scraps into rich black soil. Local gardeners line up to buy the soil for their plants.

More and more towns are collecting grass, leaves, and yard waste. Workers grind up these plant scraps for <u>mulch</u>. Gardeners spread mulch around their plants. The mulch holds in water and keeps weeds from growing. In the year 2000, for example, San Diego, California, turned 90,000 tons of yard waste into mulch.

All over America, people are finding new ways to recycle. You can help solve America's garbage problems. You can recycle paper, plastic, yard waste, and food scraps. Tell your friends and family to recycle, too. When you're shopping, look for products made of recycled materials. Together, people can turn trash into treasure and clean up the environment.

Billions of old tires are piling up around the United States. The tires are a problem. They take up a lot of space. Insect pests also lay their eggs in them.

Comprehension — Write the answers to the following questions on the lines.

1. How is plastic different from paper or yard waste in a landfill? The plastic is different from paper because most plastic is not biodegradable.

2. What are some products that can be made from recycled plastic? The some products can be made from recycled plastic were, clothing, carpets, and shoes

3. Why is recycling tires a difficult process? The recycling tires a difficult process because they need a lot of work.

Critical Thinking — Write the answers to the following questions. You will have to figure out the answers because they are not directly stated in the selection.

4. How might turning a wetland into a landfill hurt the environment? They don't like it because they want the wetland for their animals.

5. Why do you think Americans put so much trash in landfills instead of recycling it? Americans put so much trash in landfills because it take time and enrgey to do it.

Skill Focus — Read the following paragraph from the selection. It describes how tires are recycled. Write 1, 2, 3, and 4 to show the steps in order.

First, the machines chop the tires into pieces. Next, the small pieces are frozen and ground up. Big magnets then take out the steel. Finally, the machines press the rubber and plastic fibers through the holes of a metal screen. That forces the rubber away from the plastic.

__1__ Machines chop tires into pieces.

__4__ The mixture is pressed against a metal screen to separate the rubber from plastic fibers.

__3__ Big magnets take out the steel.

__2__ The small pieces of tires are frozen and ground up.

Reading-Writing Connection — Think of three things that you usually throw away. On another sheet of paper, write about how they might be recycled.

Lesson 12 Comparing and Contrasting

Reading a Science Selection

What will happen when the world runs out of oil? How will people get the power they need? This selection looks at possible ways of making energy in the future.

WORD ATTACK STRATEGIES

■ **Long Vowel Sounds**

When two vowels come together in a word, the first one usually has a **long vowel sound**. The second vowel is usually silent. For example, think about the words *wait* and *boat*. Both have two vowels that come together. In *wait*, you can hear the long *a* sound. In *boat*, you can hear the long *o* sound.

Look at the words in the box below. You will see them again in the selection.

| coal | fuel | clean | cheaper |

1. Say the words below. Circle the vowel that has the long sound in each word.

heat   grain   goal   sea

■ **Multiple-Meanings Words**

Some words have **multiple meanings**. That is, they have more than one possible meaning. For example, a word may have one meaning when it is used in everyday speech. It may have another meaning, though, when it is used in science or social studies books.

The word *cell* is an example. Its most common meaning is "a small room," such as a jail cell. In science, though, *cell* has another meaning. For example, a *cell* is "the building block of life." All plants and animals are made up of cells.

2. As you read the selection, look for a third meaning for the word *cell*. Write the meaning of *cell* as it is used in the selection.

_____

■ **Word Clues**

As you read the selection, you will see some new words. Look for clues to their meanings in nearby sentences. What clues, for example, help you figure out the meaning of the underlined word below?

> These fossil fuels are <u>nonrenewable</u>. —gone forever
> Once they are used, they are gone forever.

You may not know what *nonrenewable* means. The next sentence, however, tells you. Something that is *nonrenewable* "can be used only once—then it is gone forever."

3. As you read "Power for the Future," use word clues to figure out the meanings of the underlined words. Then use the correct word to fill in each blank in the paragraph.

sustainable   efficient   expensive

Fossil fuels are nonrenewable, but solar power is _sustainable_. Solar power is more _expensive_, or costly, than using fossil fuels. In the future, scientists hope to make solar cells more _efficient_ so that such cells will use more of the sunlight they collect.

Lesson 12 Comparing and Contrasting **41**

SKILL FOCUS

■ **Comparing and Contrasting**

Which do you like more, baseball or football? What is the funniest show on TV? In everyday life, you often compare things.

When you notice how things are alike, you **compare** them. When you see how they are different, you **contrast** them. Comparing and contrasting are good ways to learn and remember information.

Clue words help you notice comparisons and contrasts when you read. The words *like, similar, same,* and *both* are often used to point out how two things are alike. The words *different, but, however, by contrast,* and *unlike* are used to point out differences.

The paragraph below is from the selection. It contrasts energy from the sun with energy from fossil fuels such as oil.

> Solar power has many advantages. For one thing, it is clean. It does not make any air pollution. Fossil fuels, by contrast, are dirty to burn. They give off gases that are harmful to breathe. Air pollution from fossil fuels may even make the climate too warm.

You can use a chart to keep track of comparisons and contrasts. The chart below shows information from the paragraph.

Source of Energy	How Clean Is It?
Fossil Fuels (oil)	dirty to burn, give off harmful gases
Solar Power	clean, makes no air pollution

4. The next paragraph is also from the selection. It contrasts fossil fuels and solar power. Fill in the chart below to show the contrast that the paragraph makes.

> Solar power is also sustainable. We may run out of our limited fossil fuels. However, there is an unlimited supply of sunlight. We can use it forever.

Source of Energy	Amount Available
Fossil Fuels	_____
Solar Power	_____

■ **Strategy Tip** ■

As you read this selection, look for contrasts. Remember that the words *but, however, different, by contrast,* and *unlike* are often used to show differences between things.

Power for the Future

Words to Know

fossil fuels (FOS əl fyoolz)
oil, coal, and natural gas

solar power (SOHL ər POU ər)
electricity made from sunlight

air pollution (air pə LOO shən)
anything that makes air dirty

generator (JEN ər AY tər)
a machine that makes electricity

The Fossil Fuel Problem

The world has an energy problem. People depend too much on oil. They use oil to run cars and heat homes. They use it to make plastic and electricity. The people of the world use 67 million barrels of oil every day!

Why is that a problem? The amount of oil is limited. Some scientists think that more oil can be found only until the year 2010. After that, people will have to live with a lot less oil.

For a while, coal and natural gas can be used. Coal and gas, however, aren't really the answer. Like oil, coal and natural gas are **fossil fuels**. They were formed millions of years ago from dead plants and animals. These fossil fuels are nonrenewable. Once they are used, they are gone forever.

Fossil fuels have made modern life possible. Few people want to give up their cars, TVs, warm homes, and other modern things. If they want to keep these things, their goal must be to find new power sources.

Solar Power

The sun is the world's most powerful energy source. The huge fiery ball gives off more power than people could ever use. **Solar power** is electricity made from sunlight.

Solar cells are used to collect the sun's energy. Each solar cell then changes the sunlight into electricity. There are thousands of solar cells on a solar panel. A few of these solar panels can make enough electricity for a house.

Solar power has many advantages. For one thing, it is clean. It does not make any **air pollution**. Fossil fuels, by contrast, are dirty to burn. They give off gases that are harmful to breathe. Air pollution from fossil fuels may even make our climate too warm.

Solar power is also <u>sustainable</u>. The supply of fossil fuels is limited. However, there is an unlimited supply of sunlight. It can be used forever.

Solar panels like these could heat many of our homes someday.

Lesson 12 Comparing and Contrasting

There are still some problems with solar power, though. Solar cells work only on sunny days. At night or in cloudy weather, people need another power source. Solar panels also cause space problems. They are very large. Many large solar panels are needed to make lots of electricity. It would be hard to find space for them all.

Solar energy is also <u>expensive</u>. Solar panels cost a lot to build. So solar energy costs twice as much as power from fossil fuels.

Solar cells are not that <u>efficient</u> yet either. They do not use all the sunlight that hits them. Only a small amount of the light can be turned into power. The rest of the energy is wasted. People need to invent more efficient cells that do not waste so much sunlight. Then the cost of solar energy will fall.

Solar power *is* cheaper than fossil fuels in some ways, though. Air pollution from fossil fuels causes expensive damage. People get sick from breathing dirty air. Gases from burning oil also hurt plants, animals, and buildings. Solar power would save us billions of dollars in these "hidden" costs.

Wind Power

Is the answer to our energy problem blowing in the wind? Wind power is becoming more popular. People are building powerful new windmills. Some of them are more than 25 stories tall.

The science of wind power is simple. Strong winds turn blades on a windmill. These blades drive a **generator**. The generator makes electricity.

Windmills aren't right for every town, though. Some places just are not windy enough. Windmills also need lots of open space. A town would need a huge open space for its windmills.

Windmills have other problems, too. They spoil the view on open land. They also make noise and scare away wildlife.

Modern windmills are becoming much more efficient. They could supply much of our energy in the future.

Wind power is not perfect, but it could solve some of our energy problems. Today, about 1 percent of California's power comes from the wind. The breezy Midwest may make even more wind power. More farmers there are putting windmills above their fields of grain. Some day, Midwestern "wind farms" could make half of our nation's electricity.

Like solar energy, wind power is clean. It makes no pollution. Windmills are also becoming more efficient. Some make electricity from just a gentle breeze. Wind power is getting cheaper, too. It costs just a little more than power from fossil fuels.

Parts of the Solution

Solar power will be part of the answer to our fuel problem. So will wind power. Scientists may find other answers, too. Some scientists are making electricity from the waves in the sea. Others are using heat from deep inside Earth. The power of fast-moving rivers is another good source of energy. Clean energy is all around us. We just have to find ways to put it to work.

Comprehension — Write the answers to the following questions on the lines.

1. What is the "fossil fuel problem"? They are in limited supply and will run out someday.

2. What are some advantages of solar power over fossil fuels? The advantages to solar power are no air pollution and is sustainable.

Critical Thinking — Write the answers to the following questions. You will have to figure out the answers because they are not directly stated in the selection.

3. Why is air pollution considered a "hidden cost" of burning fossil fuels? Fossil fuels cause pollution and it will cost money to fix the air.

4. Why does wind power make more sense in country areas than in cities? The main reason is more space than in the country.

Skill Focus — Use details in the selection to complete the following Comparison and Contrast Chart.

	Good Features	Problems
Fossil Fuels	need it in modern life – cheap	pollution damages enviornment
Solar Power	sustainable clean safe	expensive needs alot of space
Wind Power	efficient cheap have supply	needs space noisy scares wild life

Reading-Writing Connection — How do you think people will get their power 100 years from now? On another sheet of paper, write your ideas in a paragraph.

Lesson 12 Comparing and Contrasting 45

Lesson 13 Reading Percents

Reading a Mathematics Selection

Have you ever been to a store that was having a "30 percent off" sale? What does the word *percent* (%) mean? In this selection, you will learn about percents.

WORD ATTACK STRATEGIES

■ Word Clues

As you read about percents, you will see some new words. Look for clues to their meaning in nearby sentences.

Read the following sentence. What clues help you figure out the underlined word?

> The original price of the radio was $100. On the day the store has a special sale, however, the price is <u>reduced</u> by 40%.

You may not know the word *reduced*. You probably know, however, that when stores have sales, they lower their prices. So you can figure out that *reduced* means "lowered."

As you read "Reading Percents," use word clues to figure out the meanings of the underlined words. Match each word with its meaning.

budget   money put aside for future needs

savings   a spending plan

SKILL FOCUS

■ Reading Percents

Percents are used in many parts of everyday life. A store offers a "50 percent off" sale. Banks offer 2% interest on savings accounts. What do these numbers mean?

The symbol % stands for **percent**. The word *percent* means "how many parts out of every 100." For example, *65%* means "65 parts out of a whole that has been divided into 100 equal parts." A whole is 100%.

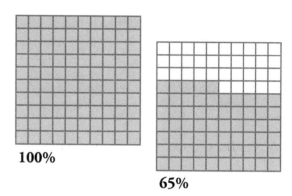

100%

65%

Percents are useful because they compare part of something to the whole. For example, Dale earned $100 cutting lawns in July. He spent $8 going to a movie. Because he spent $8 out of $100, Dale spent 8 percent, or 8%, of his money.

> ■ **Strategy Tip** ■
>
> Facts and information are often given in percents. Remember that a percent shows how many parts out of every 100 are being discussed.

46 Lesson 13 Reading Percents

Understanding Percents

Words to Know

percent (pər SENT)
how many parts out of every 100

original price (ə RIJ ə nəl preyes)
how much something cost before it went on sale

Understanding percents can help you in many ways in everyday life. You can use percents to make a <u>budget</u>, or spending plan, for your money. A budget shows what **percent** of your money you will use for different expenses. You can also use percents to make regular additions to your <u>savings</u>. Try to put aside a certain percent of your money each week or month. That way, you will have money for what you might need in the future.

A student named Dale is trying to save money from his summer job. In July, he earned $100 mowing lawns. He saved 25% of that money. How much did Dale save?

As you know, 25% means "25 parts out of every 100." If Dale saved 25% of his $100, he saved $25.

Many stores use percents on sale days. Dale notices that a store has a radio on sale. The **original price** of the radio is $100. On the day the store has a special sale, however, the price is reduced 40%. How much money does Dale need to buy the radio?

Because 40% means "40 out of every 100," Dale can save $40 if he buys the radio on sale. To find out how much the radio costs on sale, Dale subtracts $40 from the original price.

$100 − $40 = $60

Dale can buy the radio on sale for $60.

Dale buys the radio for $60. He also puts $25 in the bank as savings. What percent of the $100 that he earned does Dale have left for other expenses?

Dale's earnings were $100. He spent $60 on the radio, which is 60 out of 100, or 60%. He put $25 out of $100, or 25%, into his savings account.

60% + 25% = 85%

So far, Dale has spent and saved 85% of his money.

To find out what percent of his earnings he has left, subtract 85% from the whole. The whole of anything is always 100%.

100% − 85% = 15%

Dale has 15% of his earnings left for other expenses, or $15.

Now that you understand percents, you can use them to budget your money. Percents will also help you make decisions when you buy something on sale.

Lesson 13 Reading Percents 47

Comprehension Write the answers to the following questions on the lines.

1. What does the word *percent* mean? _____

_____

2. What are some ways in which people use percents in everyday life? _____

_____

Critical Thinking Write the answers to the following questions. You will have to figure out the answers because they are not directly stated in the selection.

3. Suppose you went into a store and saw something that was on sale for 50% off the original price. What would be an easy way to figure out the sale price? _____

_____

Skill Focus Answer the following questions. Write how you found your answers on the lines. Be sure to show the math you used.

4. Connie sees a coat for sale at her favorite store. The original price was $100. However, the store is having a sale. All coats are on sale for 25% off the original price. How much money will Connie need to buy the coat? _____

_____

5. Tamara earned $100 baby-sitting. She wants to save 20% of it. How much money will Tamara have left to spend? _____

_____

6. Tony earned $100 shoveling snow. He spent $50 on clothes and $20 on movies. What percent of his money does he have left? _____

_____

Reading–Writing Connection Suppose you have $100. On another sheet of paper, write a budget telling what percent of it you would use for different expenses.

Lesson 14 Consonant Blends

Some words have two or three consonants at the beginning. If you can hear the sounds that all the consonants stand for, this is called a **consonant blend**. Here are some two-letter blends.

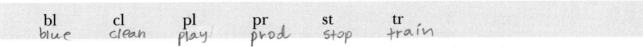

bl	cl	pl	pr	st	tr
blue	clean	play	prod	stop	train

1. Say each picture name. Listen to the consonant sounds at the beginning of each name. Then write the consonant blend that you hear.

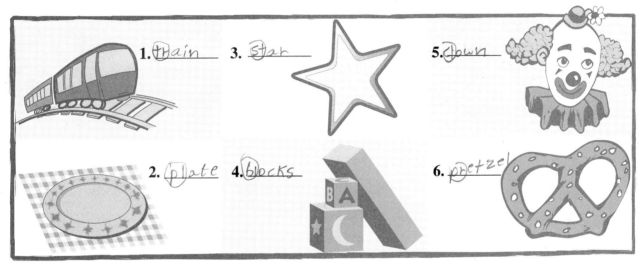

1. train
2. plate
3. star
4. blocks
5. clown
6. pretzel

Here are some three-letter blends.

scr	spl	str	spr
scream	splash	strain	sprain

2. Now say these picture names. Listen to each beginning sound. Write the blend that stands for the consonant sounds you hear.

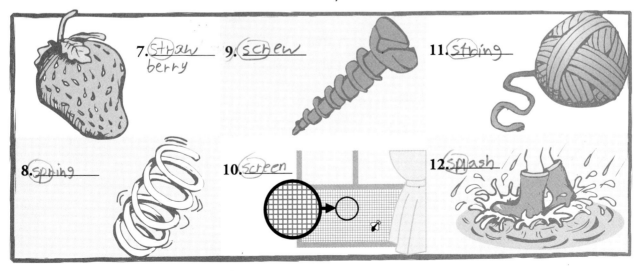

7. strawberry
8. spring
9. screw
10. screen
11. string
12. splash

Lesson 15 Long Vowel Sounds

Some words have two vowels together. The words *boat* and *eat*, for example, have two vowels together. What do you notice about the vowel sounds in these words?

| bait | sea | road | team | toast |

The first vowel in each word has a **long vowel sound**. The second vowel is silent.

Read each word below. Write the two vowels that come together. Then write which vowel has a long vowel sound.

Word	Vowels	Long Vowel Sound
1. boat	oa	o
2. wait	ai	a
3. cream	ea	e
4. peach	ea	e
5. fuel	ue	u
6. sail	ai	a
7. beach	ea	e
8. roast	oa	o

Read each sentence below. Underline the word in each sentence that has two vowels together. Say the word to yourself. Then circle the vowel that has a long vowel sound.

9. We have to cl(e)an the apartment this morning.

10. I don't mind the r(a)in very much.

11. Does Mary have a p(a)il to wash the walls?

12. Be sure that the bucket won't l(e)ak.

13. Add water and be sure to use this s(o)ap.

14. We have to p(a)int the kitchen.

15. That will be our next g(o)al.

50 Lesson 15 Long Vowel Sounds

Lesson 16 Contractions

A **contraction** is a shortened form of two words. An apostrophe (') shows where a letter or letters have been left out. Many contractions are formed with a verb and *not*.

| is + not = isn't | was + not = wasn't | could + not = couldn't |

Other contractions are formed with a pronoun and a verb.

| I + am = I'm | you + are = you're | he + is = he's |
| we + have = we've | she + had = she'd | they + will = they'll |

Write the contraction you can form from each pair of words.

1. I + am = __I'm__
2. is + not = __isn't__
3. they + have = __they've__
4. were + not = __weren't__
5. she + will = __she'll__
6. I + have = __I've__
7. did + not = __didn't__
8. do + not = __don't__
9. I + will = __I'll__
10. you + will = __you'll__
11. does + not = __doesn't__
12. he + had = __hadn't__
13. are + not = __aren't__
14. you + are = __you're__
15. they + will = __they'll__
16. was + not = __wasn't__
17. you + have = __you've__
18. could + not = __couldn't__
19. have + not = __haven't__
20. she + is = __she's__

Underline two words in each of the following sentences that can form a contraction. On the line, write the contraction.

21. <u>I have</u> always wanted to visit Washington, D.C. __I've__
22. Later today, <u>we will</u> tour the White House. __We'll__
23. <u>Do not</u> expect to see the President there, though. __Don't__
24. <u>He is</u> in Congress giving an important speech. __He's__
25. The President <u>is not</u> greeting visitors today. __isn't__

Lesson 17 Multiple-Meaning Words

Many words have **multiple meanings**. That is, they have more than one meaning. Some common words have special meanings in science and social studies. The common meaning of *bed*, for example, is "a piece of furniture to sleep on." In geography, however, a *bed* is "the bottom of a river." Similarly, the common meaning of *yard* is "the land around a house." In math, though, a *yard* is "a unit of measurement—three feet."

Below are some other words with more than one meaning. Choose the word that matches each pair of definitions below. Write it on the line provided.

| cell | pole | legend | leg | mouth |
| school | sound | line | scale | plain |

1. Common use: a place to learn
   Science: a group of fish
   __School__

2. Common use: a long, round piece of wood
   Social Studies: the point farthest north or farthest south on Earth
   __pole__

3. Common use: the opening in your head for eating and talking
   Social Studies: place where a river empties into a larger body of water
   __mouth__

4. Common use: small room in a jail
   Science: the building block of life
   __cell__

5. Common use: people standing and waiting their turn
   Math: an endless number of points that go on forever in two directions
   __line__

6. Common use: a story that may be true
   Social Studies: the key of a map
   __legend__

7. Common use: any noise
   Social Studies: part of the sea stretching between two bodies of land
   __sound__

8. Common use: part of the body used for walking
   Math: a side of a triangle
   __leg__

9. Common use: machine used to measure weight
   Science: part of the outer covering of a fish or snake
   __scale__

10. Common use: not fancy
    Social Studies: a flat, grassy area
    __plain__

Lesson 18 Reading a Graph

A **graph** shows information, or data, in a way that is easy to see and understand. Graphs use lines, bars, or circles to show information. A **double bar graph** uses two bars of different colors to compare two different sets of information.

Always read the **title** of a graph first. Then read the **labels** on the bottom and at the side. A double bar graph also has a **key** that tells you what each color on the graph stands for.

Look at the double bar graph below. It shows the heart rate for four students before and after exercise. Use the graph to answer the questions below. Fill in the circle next to the correct answer for each question.

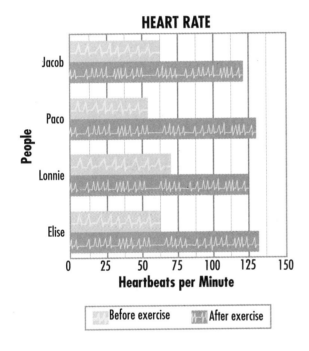

1. Which student had the slowest heart rate *after* exercise?
   - ✓ Jacob
   - ○ Paco
   - ○ Lonnie
   - ○ Elise

2. Which student had the slowest heart rate *before* exercise?
   - ○ Jacob
   - ✓ Paco
   - ○ Lonnie
   - ○ Elise

3. What was Lonnie's heart rate after exercise?
   - ○ 75 beats per minute
   - ○ 100 beats per minute
   - ✓ 125 beats per minute
   - ○ 140 beats per minute

4. How much faster was Lonnie's heartbeat after exercise compared to before exercise?
   - ○ about 25 beats per minute faster
   - ✓ about 55 beats per minute faster
   - ○ about 75 beats per minute faster
   - ○ about 100 beats per minute faster

Lesson 18 Reading a Graph 53

Lesson 19 Using a Bus Schedule

To use a bus schedule, read the **title** first. Make sure you have the right schedule for the bus you want to take.

Look at the bus schedule below. It is for a bus that runs in the town of Clifton on weekday mornings. The first row across names five places where the bus stops. The next five rows show the times when the bus stops at each place. For example, the first bus of the morning leaves Center Station at 6:10. It makes its first stop at 6:25 at the Mall and Route 125. It makes its last stop at Market and State Streets at 7:10.

Clifton Weekday Morning Bus Service				
Center Station	Mall and Route 125	River Edge	Washington Park	Market and State streets
6:10	6:25	6:40	7:00	7:10
6:40	6:55	7:10	7:30	7:40
7:10	7:25	7:40	8:00	8:10
7:40	7:55	8:10	8:30	8:40
8:10	8:25	8:40	9:00	9:10

Write the answers to the following questions on the lines provided.

1. Carlos boards the bus at Center Station at 7:10. When will he reach River Edge?
   He will reach River Edge at 7:40

2. Denise rides the bus from the Mall to Washington Park. How long is her ride?
   She will take 35 minuts

3. Joe misses the 8:10 bus at River Edge. How long must he wait for the next bus?
   He must wait for the next bus about 30 minuts

4. Toni gets on at the Mall and gets off at the next stop. How long is her bus ride?
   15 minutes

5. Connie has to be at work near Market and State streets at 8:30. Which bus should she take from River Edge so that she won't be late?
   _7:40_

UNIT 3 TIME FOR COURAGE

Lesson 20 Setting

Reading a Literature Selection

This selection tells a true story. As you read "Stop the Train," think about where and when the events happened.

WORD ATTACK STRATEGIES

■ r-Controlled Vowel Sounds

Not all vowels have a long or short sound. If the letter *r* comes after a vowel, *r* controls the sound of the vowel. The sounds of *ar, er, ir, or,* and *ur* are called **r-controlled vowel sounds.** *Tap*, for example, has a short vowel sound. *Tape* has a long vowel sound. *Tarp* has an *r*-controlled vowel sound.

Look at the words in the box. You will see them again in the selection.

barn	emergency	swirling
churning	storm	startled

1. Say these words from the story. Circle the words with an *r*-controlled vowel sound.

| her | rushed | rain | horrible |
| darkness | bridge | burst | hurried |

■ Possessive Nouns

Nouns can show ownership, or possession. Such nouns are called **possessive nouns.** Singular nouns add an apostrophe and *s* (**'s**) to show possession.

   mother of Kate = Kate**'s** mother

Plural nouns that end in *s* add only an apostrophe (') to show possession.

   lives of the travelers = travelers' lives

Plural nouns that do not end in *s* add an apostrophe and *s* (**'s**) to show possession.

   the hope of the women = the women**'s** hope

2. Rewrite each phrase using a possessive noun.

the sisters of Kate _Kate's sisters'_

the father of the girls _girls' father_

the voices of the men _men's voices_

■ Word Clues

Many stories have clues in them that help you figure out the meanings of new words. For example, what clue helps you figure out the meaning of *churning* in these sentences?

> Kate Shelley stared at the <u>churning</u> waters of Honey Creek. Heavy rains had fallen for a week. Kate had never seen so much muddy, <u>swirling water</u>. — churning

The word *swirling* can help you guess the meaning of *churning*. *Churning* means "stirring or twisting violently."

3. As you read "Stop the Train," you will see some underlined words. Look for clues to their meanings. Write the meanings below.

collapsed _____

plunged _____

perilous _____

SKILL FOCUS

■ Setting

Stories can carry you back into the past or rocket you into the future. They can take you across the country or around the world.

The **setting** of a story is the **time** and the **place** in which the action happens. Often, the author tells you the setting. At other times, you have to figure it out. You can do that by looking at details in the story.

The setting of a story often affects the plot and the characters. If two characters get lost in a forest, for example, they will have certain kinds of problems. If they get lost in a city, however, they will have different kinds of problems.

Read this paragraph from the selection. What details help you figure out the setting?

> It wouldn't be long before the flood waters reached the barn. Kate's mother kept the family's milk cow and carriage horse there. "I'm going to let the cow and horse out," Kate called to Mrs. Shelley. "That way, they can go to higher ground." Putting on her bonnet, Kate lit the barn lantern and headed outside.

You can use a Details About Setting Map like this to write down the details that help you identify the setting. Several details can help you guess the story's setting: Kate's family has a barn with a milk cow and a horse that pulls a carriage. Kate also carries a lantern. All of these details suggest that the story takes place a long time ago. The setting also seems to be in the country, perhaps near a river.

4. Now read the following paragraph. Underline the details that help you identify the setting. Then write the time and place of the setting on the lines.

> The Shelley house stood beside Honey Creek, near Moingona, Iowa. Just past Kate's house, Honey Creek emptied into the Des Moines River. Muddy waters from the creek and the river were inching ever closer that July night. Should Kate, her mother, and her sisters leave the house? Kate's father had died three years before, in 1878. Ever since, 15-year-old Kate had helped her mother care for the family.

Time: _July_

Place: _Honey Creek_

- Detail: barn with a milk cow and horse
- Detail: Kate carries lantern
- Detail: Kate put on her bonnet
- Detail: Flood waters reaching the barn

SETTING

■ Strategy Tip ■

Remember that the setting includes both the time and the place of the story. When you read, think about how the setting affects the characters and events.

Stop the Train

Words to Know

passengers (PAS ən jərz)
people who travel in a train, bus, ship, or car

schedule (SKEJ ul)
a list of times when certain events are planned to happen

emergency (i MER jən see)
an unexpected situation that calls for fast action

delay (də LAY)
to cause someone or something to be late

Lightning flashed, thunder boomed, and the rains poured down. From her kitchen window, Kate Shelley stared at the churning waters of Honey Creek. Heavy rains had fallen for a week. Kate had never seen so much muddy, swirling water.

It wouldn't be long before the flood waters reached the barn. Kate's mother kept the family's milk cow and carriage horse there. "I'm going to let the cow and horse out," Kate said to Mrs. Shelley. "That way, they can go to higher ground." Putting on her bonnet, Kate lit the barn lantern and headed outside.

The Shelley house stood beside Honey Creek, near Moingona, Iowa. Just past Kate's house, Honey Creek emptied into the Des Moines River. Muddy waters from the creek and the river were inching ever closer that July night. Should Kate, her mother, and her sisters leave the house? Kate's father had died three years before, in 1878. Ever since, 15-year-old Kate had helped her mother care for the family.

The wail of a steam engine cut through the storm. In the distance, a single engine crossed the Des Moines River Bridge. Kate watched its shadow move closer. Soon, it would cross nearby Honey Creek Bridge.

The flood waters, however, had weakened Honey Creek Bridge. Its old wooden frame began to sway as soon as the steam engine started across. When the train reached the halfway point, the bridge bent under its weight. Then the wood began to split. Finally, the bridge collapsed, breaking completely apart. For a second, the engine hung in the air. Then, with an ugly hiss, it plunged into 20 feet of water. As it fell, Kate watched in horror.

"The bridge collapsed!" she shouted to her mother. "An engine went down. I've got to tell the station."

"But in this storm . . . ," Mrs. Shelley said in a worried voice.

"I have to warn them," Kate insisted. "A train full of **passengers** is due here." Living next to the tracks, Kate knew the **schedule** of the few trains that passed each day. "If I don't warn the station, the passenger train might try to use the bridge!"

"There isn't time," Mrs. Shelley replied. "The station is a mile away!"

"It's an **emergency**!" Kate said. "I've got to try. If I don't, the passengers could die!"

Grabbing the lantern, Kate raced out into the storm. The station was a mile to the west. The only way to get there quickly was to cross the Des Moines River Bridge.

The bridge was built for trains, not people. It was little more than two steel rails stretched across narrow, wooden strips. The strips were spaced so far apart that Kate could easily fall between them. There were no handrails.

There was no place to go if a train should come. Even on a sunny day, the bridge was dangerous for a person to cross.

Desperately hoping that the storm would **delay** the passenger train, Kate climbed onto the bridge. The water below roared. The whistling wind took her breath away. She had never before tried to do anything so dangerous. Getting down on her hands and knees, she began her perilous crossing. *(not safe)*

A gust of wind quickly blew out the lantern. Kate had to feel her way in the darkness. Foot by foot she crept, with the rough, wooden strips scraping her legs.

With a loud swoosh, a huge tree suddenly swept down the river. It was so big that its top branches hit the bridge, almost knocking Kate off. A spray of water and mud drenched her clothes.

On and on she crept, for what seemed like hours. Every moment, she expected to hear the rumble of the passenger train. Then, finally, her fingers clutched cold rocks. She was safely across the river!

On wobbly legs, Kate hurried to the station. Wet and covered with mud, she burst through the door. "Honey Creek Bridge is out!" she shouted to the startled stationmaster. "Stop the passenger train!" Then, exhausted, she fell to the floor.

The passenger train was nearing the station. It was not scheduled to stop there, though. So the stationmaster rushed out onto the tracks with a lantern. He was just in time to stop the train.

As time passed, Kate Shelley wanted only to forget that horrible night. Many people, however, remembered her bravery. The railroad workers gave her a gold watch. The passengers on the train collected money so she could go to college. People from all over the United States sent her gifts.

Years later, after Kate became a teacher, a new bridge was built across the Des Moines River. The bridge needed a name.

"Let's name it the Kate Shelley Bridge," someone suggested. Others quickly agreed. That way, people would always remember the brave girl who risked her life to stop the train and saved so many people.

Comprehension — Write the answers to the following questions on the lines.

1. Why did the Honey Creek Bridge collapse? _The Honey Creek Bridge collapsed_ _because of heavy rains had fallen for a week and storm._

2. Why did Kate have to hurry to the station during the storm? _Kate had to hurry_ _to station during the storm because she wanted to save the passengers on the train._

3. How do you know that people appreciated Kate's bravery? _People appreciated Kate's_ _bravery by gave her a gold watch, collected money for her college and_ _they named the bridge after her._

Critical Thinking — Write the answers to the following questions. You will have to figure out the answers because they are not directly stated in the selection.

4. Do you think Kate Shelley was a hero? Explain why or why not. _Yes, I think she_ _was a hero because of what she has done to save people._

5. Suppose the story were set in the present. How might Kate have warned the stationmaster about the bridge collapse? _If this happened in present day I would_ _use the phone._

Skill Focus — In the circles, write details about the dangerous setting on the Des Moines River Bridge as Kate tried to cross it.

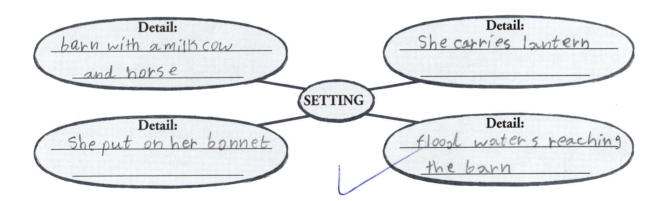

- Detail: barn with a milk cow and horse
- Detail: She carries lantern
- Detail: She put on her bonnet
- Detail: flood waters reaching the barn

SETTING

Reading-Writing Connection — Suppose you are Kate. On another sheet of paper, write a short diary entry you might have written on the night the bridge collapsed.

Lesson 20 Setting 59

Lesson 21   Fact and Opinion

Reading a Social Studies Selection

A code is a secret form of writing or talking. During a war, codes are important. They keep information secret. In this selection, you will read about a code the United States used in World War II.

WORD ATTACK STRATEGIES

■ **Silent Letters** *k* and *w*

Some words begin with **silent letters**. A silent letter has no sound in a particular word. For example, you cannot hear the sound of the letter *k* in the word *know*. The *w* in the word *wring* is also silent. Knowing which letters are silent will help you read many words.

Look at the words in the box. You will see them again in the selection.

| kneeling | wrecked | written | knew |

1. Say the words below. Draw a line through the silent letter in each word.

| knob | wrist | knit |
| wrong | knot | wrap |

■ **Suffixes**

A **suffix** is a word part that is added to the end of a base word. A suffix adds to the meaning of a base word. The chart below shows three common suffixes.

Suffix	Meaning	Example
-ful	full of	hope<u>ful</u>
-ly	in a certain way	bad<u>ly</u>
-er	one who does	work<u>er</u>

2. The words below are from the selection. Underline the suffix in each word.

skillful	luckily	talker
bomber	successful	slowly
highly	useful	breaker

■ **Word Clues**

As you read the selection, you will see new words. Try to figure out what they mean. The details in nearby sentences will help you. What clues in the sentences below help you figure out the meaning of the underlined word?

> The U.S. government <u>recruited</u> about 400 Navajos. The government convinced the Navajos to join the Marines.

You may not know the word *recruited*, but the words "convinced the Navajos to join" are clues to its meaning. *Recruited* means "convinced someone to join."

3. As you read "The Code Talkers," try to figure out the meanings of the underlined words. Match each word with its meaning.

impressed	said someone was good or valuable
contributed	strongly affected
praised	gave

SKILL FOCUS

■ Fact and Opinion

Sometimes, writers give information about a topic. At other times, they write about their feelings and judgments. Being able to tell the difference between information and judgments is important. This skill will help you judge the truth of what you read.

A **fact** is information about something. Facts can be proved true or false. For example, you could check the facts below in a history book. Other sources would also show these facts to be true.

> World War II began in 1941 for the United States. In that year, the United States went to war against Japan and Germany.

An **opinion** is what a person thinks or feels about something. It cannot be proved true or false. Opinions are often expressed with words such as *best, worst, should, think, very, probably, perhaps,* and *deserves*. Words like these show feelings and judgments. The sentences below express the writer's opinions about World War II.

> Fighting Japan was one of the hardest jobs the United States would ever face. Japan's soldiers were fierce fighters. They were very well trained for war.

The sentences above are opinions. The words *hardest, fierce,* and *very well* show feelings and judgments. Before you accept an opinion, look for facts that support it. Then decide whether you agree or disagree with the writer based on the facts.

4. Decide whether each sentence below is a fact or an opinion. Write *fact* or *opinion* on the line.

_____ The Japanese were the best code breakers in the world.

_____ Before 1942, Japan had figured out every code the Americans made up.

_____ In 1942, a new American code went into use.

_____ Navajo is a very difficult language to learn.

5. In this selection, you will learn many facts about the Navajo code talkers. After you read the selection, write your own opinion of the code talkers. Give two facts from the selection to support your opinion.

My opinion: _____

_____

Fact 1: _____

Fact 2: _____

■ **Strategy Tip** ■

As you read the selection, look for the facts and opinions the writer has included. Think about which statements can be proved. Look for statements that show the writer's feelings and judgments.

Lesson 21 Fact and Opinion

The Code Talkers

Words to Know

invaded (in VAYD əd)
entered with force

reservation (rez er VAY shən)
an area of land set aside for special use by the government

enemy (EN ə mee)
a person or group that tries to harm another person or group

military (MIL ə TAIR ee)
having to do with the armed forces and soldiers

World War II began in 1941 for the United States. In that year, the United States went to war against Japan and Germany. Japan's army had **invaded** many countries in Asia. The Japanese had taken over the Philippines. They also held other islands in the Pacific Ocean.

Fighting Japan was one of the hardest jobs the United States would ever face. Japan's soldiers were fierce fighters. They were very well trained for war.

The Japanese were also the best code breakers in the world. Before 1942, Japan had figured out every code the Americans had made up. When Americans sent secret messages by radio, the Japanese listened. They always knew what the Americans were planning. As a result, American ships were wrecked, and many lives were lost. American efforts to break the Japanese codes were not as successful.

In 1942, a new American code went into use. Japan's code breakers went to work. For three years, they worked on the code. However, they never broke it.

The Navajo Code

A man named Philip Johnston had the idea for the new code. He grew up on a Navajo (NAV ə hoh) **reservation** in Arizona. Johnston spoke Navajo. He knew that very few people in the world spoke the language. He thought that a secret code based on the Navajo language would be unbreakable.

With Johnston's help, the U.S. government recruited about 400 Navajos. The government convinced the Navajos to join the Marines. These men and women learned to be "code talkers."

The code talkers were soon fighting in the Pacific. They spoke coded messages on the phones and radios. They sent orders that told the Marines where to go. They called in ships and bombers. The Navajo code let Marines in different places talk to each other. **Enemy** soldiers could hear the Navajo code on the radio. They just couldn't break it!

These Navajo "code talkers" helped the U.S. Marines win many battles during World War II.

Why was the Navajo code so hard to break? For one thing, Navajo is not a written language. It has no alphabet. In addition, only a handful of people around the world could speak the language. No one in Japan spoke Navajo.

Navajo is a very difficult language to learn. A Navajo word can have many different meanings. The meaning depends on the speaker's tone of voice.

The code talkers did not speak ordinary Navajo either. They made up code words to describe **military** objects. For example, the Navajos did not have a word for *battleship*. So, they used their word for "whale." The Navajos also had no word for *bombs*. So, they used a word that means "bird eggs."

The Navajos worked hard to learn the code. One wrong message could cost many lives. They became very skillful at their jobs. In all, they learned more than 400 code words. The chart below shows a few of them.

English Word	Navajo Word	Navajo Meaning
submarine	BESH-LO	iron fish
destroyer	CA-LO	shark
fighter plane	DA-HI-TIH-HI	hummingbird
spy plane	NE-AS-JAH	owl
general	BIH-KEH-HE	war chief

The Navajos also made up a code alphabet. For each English letter, they used a Navajo word. For the letter *a*, they used their word for "ant." The letter *b* was their word for "bear." *C* was the Navajo word for "cat," and so on. This alphabet was highly useful. It let the code talkers spell the names of people and islands.

Helping Win the War

From island to island, the U.S. Marines slowly crossed the Pacific Ocean. On each island, terrible fighting took place. The Navajo code talkers were in every battle. Kneeling on beaches and in jungles, they operated the radios and phones.

Perhaps their most important service was in the battle at Iwo Jima (EE woh JEE muh). Iwo Jima is a small island belonging to Japan. A bloody battle took place there in February 1945. More than 6,800 Americans died on that island. About 15,000 Japanese soldiers died.

The battle was an important victory for the Americans. The Navajo code talkers played an important part in the battle. In two days, they sent and received 800 secret messages. They did not make one mistake.

Their work had a strong effect on Major Howard Conner, an officer in the U.S. Marines. He was very impressed by the code talkers' heroic work. "Were it not for the Navajo code talkers," he claimed, "the Marines would never have taken Iwo Jima."

After the War

In 1945, the war finally ended. Back in the United States, many soldiers told war stories. The code talkers, however, had to keep quiet. The Navajo code was still a military secret. The United States thought it might need the code again. Few Americans knew how much the code talkers had contributed by giving their special skills to the Marines.

More than 25 years passed. In 1971, the U.S. government finally honored the code talkers. President Nixon and Congress praised the Navajos, telling them how valuable their service had been. Today, all Americans honor the Navajo code talkers.

Comprehension Write the answers to the following questions on the lines.

1. In what important way is the Navajo language different from English? _____

_____

2. Look at the code chart on page 63. What Navajo word stands for *destroyer*? What does the

   Navajo word actually mean? _____

3. After the war, why did the code talkers have to keep silent about their work in the war?

_____

Critical Thinking Write the answers to the following questions. You will have to figure out the answers because they are not directly stated in the selection.

4. Why is it important to keep military information secret in times of war? _____

_____

_____

5. How might the battle at Iwo Jima have been different if the Japanese had broken the

   Navajo code? _____

_____

Skill Focus On the lines below, write two facts from the selection. Then write two opinions from the selection.

6. Fact: _____

7. Fact: _____

8. Opinion: _____

_____

9. Opinion: _____

_____

Reading–Writing Connection On another sheet of paper, describe a code you might invent. Tell how you could use it.

Lesson 21 Fact and Opinion

Lesson 22 Cause and Effect

Reading a Science Selection

What lies beyond Earth? Each year, a few brave people board the space shuttle to find out. In this selection, you will learn more about the shuttle.

WORD ATTACK STRATEGIES

■ Silent Letters *gh*

Some words have **silent letters**. Some silent letters are at the beginning of words, such as *k* in *know* and *w* in *wrong*. Other silent letters are in the middle or at the end of words, such *gh* in *bought* and *gh* in *high*. Knowing which letters are silent will help you read many words.

Look at the words in the box. You will see them again in the selection.

| though | weight | flight |

1. Say the words below. Circle the silent letters in each word.

weigh   caught   dough

■ Prefixes

A **prefix** is a word part that is added to the beginning of a base word. A prefix adds to the meaning of a base word. Three common prefixes are shown below.

Prefix	Meaning	Example
pre-	before	<u>pre</u>heat
re-	again	<u>re</u>write
un-	not	<u>un</u>happy

Look at the words below. You will see them again in the selection.

| reused | preplanned | uncovered |

2. Read each of the following words. Underline the prefix in each word.

unsure   rewind   prepaid
review   preschool   unusual

■ Word Clues

As you read, try to figure out the meanings of new words. Clues in nearby sentences can help you. What clues help you figure out the meaning of the underlined word below?

> Inside the orbiter are the shuttle's crew and its <u>cargo</u>, the valuable materials it carries.

You may not know what *cargo* means. However, the end of the sentence tells you the word's meaning. *Cargo* is "the valuable materials carried in a vehicle."

3. As you read "The Space Shuttle," look for clues to the meanings of the underlined words. Fill in the correct words in the blanks in the paragraph below.

| modules | atmosphere | gravity |

There is no _____ in space, so the space shuttle must carry its own air supply. There is no _____ in space, so the crew members are weightless and can float around the ship. The ship carries _____ that the crew uses to build a space station.

SKILL FOCUS

■ Cause and Effect

Why is your favorite baseball team losing so many games? Why is that new TV show so popular? Why is a space shuttle flight being delayed? Writers often tell why things happen the way they do.

An **effect** is something that happens. A **cause** is why something happens. When one thing causes another thing to happen, we say there is a **cause-and-effect** relationship between the events.

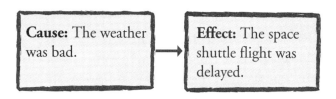

Looking for causes and effects will help you understand the events you read about. One way to do that is to ask yourself, "What happened?" The answer will be the *effect*. You can also ask yourself, "Why did that event happen?" Then you will find the *cause*.

Read the following sentences. Can you find the cause and the effect?

> For space travel to be practical, a reusable spacecraft was needed. So the United States built the first space shuttle.

If you ask, "What happened?" the answer is clear: *The United States built the first space shuttle.* That is the effect.

If you ask, "Why did it happen?" you will find the cause: *A reusable spacecraft was needed.*

Sometimes, writers use clue words or phrases such as *because, so,* and *as a result* to show causes and effects. In the following sentences, the word *so* signals that the writer is about to explain an effect.

The orbiter's rockets are not strong enough to lift it into space, though. **So** two booster rockets help with the liftoff.

4. Find the cause and the effect in the passage below. Write them on the lines.

> The astronauts also put the Hubble Telescope into a higher orbit. As a result, the telescope is now sending clearer pictures back to Earth.

Cause: _____

_____

_____

Effect: _____

_____

_____

■ Strategy Tip ■

As you read, look for examples of causes and effects. To find an effect, ask, "What happened?" To find a cause, ask, "Why did it happen?"

---

66 Lesson 22 Cause and Effect

The Space Shuttle

Words to Know

orbits (OR bits)
moves in a curved path around a planet or star

satellite (SAT əl eyet)
an object that moves in a curved path around a heavenly body

astronauts (AS trə nawts)
people who are trained to fly spaceships

telescope (TEL ə skohp)
an instrument that makes distant objects appear nearer and larger

The space shuttle is an amazing machine. It blasts off like a rocket. It **orbits** Earth like a **satellite**. Then, flying back to Earth, it lands like an airplane.

The first shuttle flew in 1981. It changed space travel forever. Before then, spaceships were used only once. After one flight, they were too damaged to be reused.

For space travel to be practical, a reusable spacecraft was needed. So the United States built the first space shuttle. Two of the shuttle's three main parts can be used again.

The Parts of the Space Shuttle

The main part of the space shuttle is the orbiter. Inside the orbiter are the shuttle's crew and its cargo, the valuable materials it carries. The orbiter reaches space and orbits Earth. Then it returns to Earth.

Three rocket engines power the orbiter. The orbiter's rockets are not strong enough to lift it into space, though. So two rocket boosters help with the liftoff. Two minutes after liftoff, the rocket boosters fall away. They are picked up and reused.

The largest part of the shuttle is the fuel tank. It is more than 150 feet long. The rockets burn the fuel in this tank during the first eight minutes of liftoff. When it is empty, the unneeded fuel tank drops away.

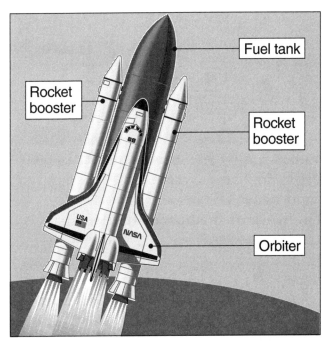

The orbiter and the rocket boosters of the space shuttle can be reused many times. The fuel tank cannot.

The Space Shuttle Crew

The space shuttle can carry seven people. The commander is in charge of the spacecraft. The pilot helps the commander. Each flight also has mission specialists. These people have trained to do special jobs during the flight.

The commander, the pilot, and the mission specialists are **astronauts**. Other crew members are not. They may be scientists or doctors. Their job is to run special equipment or do experiments.

Shuttle astronauts, high above Earth's surface, place a satellite into orbit.

The Work of the Space Shuttle

The crew members do many special jobs. Sometimes the astronauts put a new satellite into orbit. Sometimes they repair an older satellite.

In 1990, a space shuttle put the Hubble Telescope into orbit. This orbiting **telescope** is the size of a school bus. The Hubble has a much better view of space than telescopes on Earth do. It has uncovered new stars in outer space.

In 1993, 1997, and 2002 the shuttle astronauts returned to the Hubble Telescope. They replaced some worn-out parts. The astronauts also put the Hubble Telescope into a higher orbit. As a result, the telescope is now sending clearer pictures back to Earth. You can see many of these amazing photos at the NASA Web site.

On some flights, the shuttle carries a science room called Spacelab. Astronauts and scientists do experiments in this lab. Often, the scientists explore how life in space affects people.

Shuttle crews are also helping to build the International Space Station. They are using 100 sections, or modules. Each module is assembled on Earth. Then the shuttle carries the modules into space.

Shuttle astronauts began the work in 1999. When they are done in 2006, the International Space Station will be the size of a football field. Teams of scientists will live and work there.

Life on the Space Shuttle

Most space shuttle missions last from seven to ten days. The flight plan shows what each crew member will do each day. Each job has been carefully planned before the astronauts leave Earth. The astronauts practice their jobs before takeoff. They know exactly what to do in space.

Tasks that are simple on Earth are difficult in space. For example, there is no atmosphere in space. That means there is no air to breathe. So fresh oxygen must be pumped through the shuttle.

There is also very little water on the shuttle. When the astronauts breathe out, there is water in their breath. This water is collected and recycled.

Each astronaut can bring only one or two small personal items on a mission. The reason is that there is very little room inside the space shuttle.

In the space shuttle, everything is weightless. If an astronaut drops a tool, it does not fall to the ground. It floats through the air. Even a spilled drink floats through the air as drops of liquid.

Astronauts find special ways to deal with weightlessness. They clip their sleeping bags to the cabin walls. That way, sleeping astronauts will not float off. They keep their drinks in sealed packs that cannot leak. Tape holds their food trays to the table. Some astronauts even put sticky sauces on their foods. The sauce causes the food to stick to the plate, instead of floating away.

The Space Shuttle Returns

During a mission, the shuttle is at least 200 miles above Earth. It moves at 17,500 miles per hour. When it is time to return to Earth, the shuttle has to slow down and drop out of its orbit.

To slow down, the pilot swings the shuttle around. The rocket engines slow the craft down, because they are now firing backward. When the shuttle has slowed to 1,700 miles per hour, the pilot swings it around again. This points its nose forward again. Now the shuttle is about 60 miles above Earth.

Soon the shuttle glides into Earth's atmosphere. The astronauts begin to feel the force of Earth's <u>gravity</u>. They are no longer weightless.

Speeding through Earth's atmosphere causes the shuttle to heat up. Parts of the ship glow red-hot. Special tiles on the shuttle protect the crew from the high heat.

The commander and the pilot steer the shuttle toward the landing strip. The shuttle touches down softly. Because it takes a while to get used to gravity again, the astronauts do not come out of the orbiter right away. They stay inside until they once again feel comfortable with the effects of gravity. When they leave the orbiter, their mission is complete.

The shuttle orbiter lands on a runway, just as an airplane does. A parachute helps it to stop.

The Future of the Space Shuttle

The space shuttle has a great future. It allows us to explore outer space and make new discoveries. Thanks to the shuttle, the International Space Station will soon be working.

The shuttle might take more people to the moon. The moon has many natural resources. There may be new sources of energy there, too. The shuttle can help people find these resources and bring them back for use on Earth. This is just one of the ways that space shuttle crews are helping prepare the people of Earth for the challenges of the future.

Comprehension — Write the answers to the following questions on the lines.

1. How is the space shuttle different from earlier U.S. spacecraft? _____

2. What are some jobs that shuttle astronauts do? _____

3. What does the pilot of the shuttle do first when it is time to slow down and drop out of orbit? _____

Critical Thinking — Write the answers to the following questions. You will have to figure out the answers because they are not directly stated in the selection.

4. Why do you think the author wrote this article about the space shuttle? _____

5. Why do you think many people would like to travel on the space shuttle? _____

Skill Focus — Draw a line to match each cause with its effect. Look for what happened (the effect) and why it happened (the cause).

Cause

6. It takes a while to get used to gravity.
7. Speeding through the atmosphere heats up the shuttle.
8. There is no atmosphere in space.

Effect

a. Parts of the spacecraft glow red-hot.
b. Fresh oxygen must be pumped through the shuttle.
c. When they land, the astronauts don't come out of the orbiter right away.

Reading-Writing Connection — Do you think that exploring space is important? On another sheet of paper, write a paragraph to share your ideas.

70 Lesson 22 Cause and Effect

Lesson 23 Reading Metric Terms

Reading a Mathematics Selection

Have you ever bought a 2-liter bottle of juice? Have you ever run in a 100-meter dash? Metric measurements are becoming more common. In this selection, you will learn about the metric system.

WORD ATTACK STRATEGIES

■ Word Clues

As you read about metric measurement, you will see some new words. Look for clues to their meanings in nearby sentences.

Read the following sentences. What clues help you figure out the meaning of the underlined word?

> To change a measurement in a large metric unit to a measurement in a smaller unit, multiply. Suppose, for example, you wanted to <u>convert</u> 5 kilometers to meters.

You may not know the word *convert*. In the sentence before, however, the word *change* is a clue. To *convert* units means "to change from one kind of measurement to another."

As you read "Going Metric," use word clues to figure out the meanings of the underlined words. Then answer the two questions below.

What metric <u>units</u> are used to measure weight? _____

What are some metric measurements of <u>distance</u>? _____

SKILL FOCUS

■ Reading Metric Terms

The **metric system** of measurement is used in most countries. It is an easy system to use because it is based on the number 10. Most everyday measurements can be made with three metric units.

To measure length, use the **meter**. A meter is about the length of a baseball bat.

To measure weight, use the **gram**. A gram is about the weight of a dollar bill.

To measure volume, use the **liter**. A liter of milk is about as much as a quart of milk.

The more you use the metric system, the easier it seems. For now, just remember what each unit measures and how the amounts compare to other measurements you know.

■ Strategy Tip ■

Remember the three basic units of the metric system: the meter (length), the gram (weight), and the liter (volume).

Going Metric

Words to Know

meter (MEE tər)
the basic unit of length in the metric system

kilometer (kə LAH mə tər)
1,000 meters

Have you ever heard of a race called the 100-meter dash? Today, many track and field events are measured in **meters** and **kilometers**, not yards and miles. Metric measurements such as these are becoming more common in the United States.

Look closely at the word *kilometer*. It is made up of two parts: the prefix *kilo-* and the base word *meter*. The prefix *kilo-* means "1,000." A kilometer equals 1,000 meters.

All metric measurements are based on three units, or standard amounts: the meter, the gram, and the liter. To express larger or smaller amounts, prefixes are added to make the unit 10 times, 100 times, or 1,000 times larger or smaller. Study the chart below to find out some standard metric measures.

Prefix	Meaning	Examples
kilo-	1,000	kilometer, kilogram
centi-	100	centimeter, centiliter
milli-	1,000	milliliter, millimeter

Suppose you want to convert 5 kilometers to meters. To do that, follow these steps.

Rule: To change a measurement in a large metric unit to a measurement in a smaller unit, multiply.

Step 1: Choose the fact you need.

1 kilometer = 1,000 meters

Step 2: Decide whether to multiply or divide. To change a measurement in a large unit to a measurement in a smaller unit, multiply.

Step 3: Multiply.

5 kilometers x 1,000 = 5,000 meters

5 kilometers is the same as 5,000 meters.

Suppose the distance, or length, from your home to your school is 3,700 meters. If you run to school from your home, how many kilometers do you run?

Rule: To change a measurement in a smaller metric unit to a measurement in a larger one, divide.

Step 1: Choose the fact you need.

1 kilometer = 1,000 meters

Step 2: Decide whether to multiply or divide. To change a measurement in a smaller unit to a measurement in a larger unit, divide.

Step 3: Divide.

3,700 meters ÷ 1,000 = 3.7 kilometers

The distance from home to school is 3.7 kilometers.

You can use these three steps to work with other metric units, too. For example, you can change a measurement in grams to kilograms or milligrams. With a little practice, you will be ready to go metric in no time.

Comprehension Write the answers to the following questions on t...

1. What are the three steps for changing a measurement in one metric unit to another metric unit?

Step 1: _____

Step 2: _____

Step 3: _____

2. Which metric unit is 100 times smaller than a meter? _____

Critical Thinking Write the answer to the following question. You will have to figure out the answer because it is not directly stated in the selection.

3. For many years, the United States did not use the metric system. Why do you think it is being used more today? _____

Skill Focus Use the three steps to solve the following word problems.

4. A jogger ran 4 kilometers one morning. How many meters did she run?

Step 1: _____

Step 2: _____

Step 3: _____

5. At a track meet, a student won a 2,500-meter race. How many kilometers long was the race?

Step 1: _____

Step 2: _____

Step 3: _____

Reading-Writing Connection On another sheet of paper, write a word problem that involves changing a measurement in one metric unit to another unit.

...olled Vowel Sounds

...r short sound. If the letter *r* comes after a
...und of the vowel. The sounds of *ar, er, ir, or,*
...**lled vowel sounds**.

...self: *cap, cape, carp*. The word *cap* has a short
...*cape* has a long vowel sound. The word *carp* has
...sound.

Read ... words below. Underline the word with an *r*-controlled vowel sound.

1. cut curt cute
2. ban barn bane
3. can cane car
4. chart chat chain
5. hen her heat

6. bird bide bid
7. code cod cord
8. chip chirp chime
9. torn toad top
10. tub tube turn

Now say the words below. Each word has one vowel sound. Listen for the vowel sound. On the line, write whether the vowel sound is *long, short,* or *r-controlled*.

11. term _____
12. curl _____
13. grate _____
14. tap _____
15. brain _____

16. drum _____
17. star _____
18. shirt _____
19. chin _____
20. hurt _____

Read each sentence. Underline the word with an *r*-controlled vowel sound in each sentence.

21. We saw a fox at the farm last night.
22. It was about two feet long, with red fur.
23. The fox ran through the yard and out into the fields.
24. Its bushy tail ended in a long black curl.
25. It left its tracks in the soft dirt by the apple trees.

Lesson 25 Silent Letters

Many English words have one or more silent letters. A **silent letter** makes no sound when you say the word. For example, you don't say the *k* sound in the word *know*. The letter *k* is silent.

Some silent letters are at the beginning of words.

Words that begin with *kn* have a silent *k*.

| know | knew | kneel |

Words that begin with *wr* have a silent *w*.

| wrong | wrap | wren |

Sometimes, the letters *gh* are silent. The silent letters *gh* can appear in the middle or at the end of words.

| weight | caught | high | bough |

Read each word. Draw a line through the silent letter or letters.

1. wrist
2. fight
3. wrestle
4. knit
5. wrench
6. knot
7. wreck
8. bought
9. knob
10. although
11. wrapper
12. knight
13. wring
14. taught
15. known

Read each sentence. Circle the silent letters *k*, *w*, and *gh* each time you see them.

16. Lost in a storm at night, a sailboat turned into the wrong bay.
17. Sharp rocks cut through the wooden ship like knives.
18. In the lighthouse, a young man knew he must do something.
19. With his knees shaking, he rowed out into the storm to reach the wreck.
20. There, kneeling down in his boat, he grabbed the sailors by the wrists and pulled them into the rowboat.

Possessive Nouns

A noun names a person, place, idea, or thing. A noun can also show ownership, or possession. The underlined nouns below are **possessive nouns**.

We went to Jason's garage sale.
We visited the artists' studio.
The highlight was the children's parade.

Follow these rules to form possessive nouns.

To form the possessive of a singular noun, add an apostrophe and s ('s).

    a child's game   Bill's job   James's report

To form the possessive of a plural noun that ends in s, add only an apostrophe (').

    many students' books   two girls' coats   the workers' jobs

To form the possessive of a plural noun that does not end in s, add an apostrophe and s ('s).

    the geese's feathers   the children's playground   many people's hopes

Use a possessive noun to rewrite each phrase. Before you write, decide whether the noun is singular or plural.

1. the book belonging to the girl _____
2. the coats belonging to the guests _____
3. the mother of Kyle _____
4. the house belonging to the men _____
5. the flavor of the blackberries _____
6. the home of Mrs. Jones _____
7. food for the mice _____
8. the design on the glass _____
9. the toys belonging to the children _____
10. the bikes belonging to the girls _____

Lesson 27 Prefixes and Suffixes

A **prefix** is a word part that is added to the beginning of a base word. A **suffix** is a word part that is added to the end of a base word. Both prefixes and suffixes add to the meaning of a base word.

Three common prefixes, their meanings, and their examples are shown below.

Prefix	Meaning	Examples
pre-	before	preheat, prepay
re-	again	redo, rewind
un-	not, the opposite of	unhappy, untie

Three common suffixes, their meanings, and their examples are shown below.

Suffix	Meaning	Examples
-ful	full of	thoughtful, wonderful
-ly	in a certain way	slowly, happily
-er	one who does	worker, painter

Add a prefix or suffix to each word below. The new word should have the meaning given.

1. ___ happy   "not happy"
2. build ___   "one who builds"
3. ___ war   "before a war"
4. joy ___   "full of joy"
5. kind ___   "in a kind way"
6. ___ locked   "not locked"
7. ___ learn   "learn again"
8. sad ___   "in a sad way"
9. ___ game   "before a game"
10. hunt ___   "one who hunts"

Underline the words that contain a prefix or suffix from the boxes above. Circle the prefix or suffix in each underlined word.

11. One day, a youthful black bear walked nervously through a New Jersey shopping center.
12. Some shoppers in the preholiday crowd screamed wildly.
13. Others calmly called the state's animal control officers.
14. Officials drugged the bear so that they could relocate it to a heavily wooded area.
15. When the bear reawakened, it seemed comfortable in its unfamiliar surroundings.
16. Workers say it ran off in the predawn light and has not come back to the city.

Reading a Table

...studies books, you will often see **tables**. Tables ... so that they are easy to find. In a table, words ... in rows and columns.

... its **title**. The title tells you what kinds of facts are ... the **headings** of the columns and rows. The ... own. The rows run from left to right. Finally, look ... across the rows to find the facts you need.

Use this table to answer the questions below.

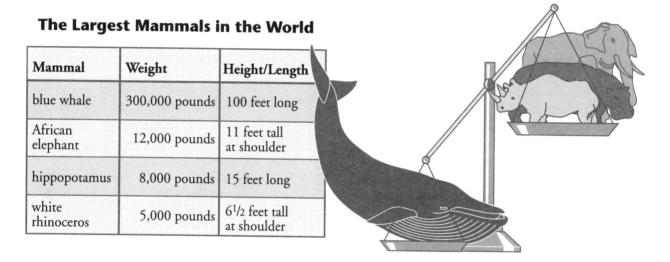

The Largest Mammals in the World

Mammal	Weight	Height/Length
blue whale	300,000 pounds	100 feet long
African elephant	12,000 pounds	11 feet tall at shoulder
hippopotamus	8,000 pounds	15 feet long
white rhinoceros	5,000 pounds	6½ feet tall at shoulder

1. What is the title of the table? _____
2. What is the heading of the second column? _____
3. What animal is described in the last row? _____
4. How long is a blue whale? _____
5. How much does a hippopotamus weigh? _____
6. Which animal weighs the least? Fill in the circle next to the correct answer.

○ blue whale   ○ African elephant
○ hippopotamus   ○ white rhinoceros

Lesson 29 Using the Yellow Pages

The **Yellow Pages** are a section of the telephone book. It lists the businesses in your area. Use the Yellow Pages to find the names, numbers, and addresses of local businesses.

The Yellow Pages have headings to group businesses. All of the [same kind] of businesses are listed under the same heading. For example, [dentists] are listed under the heading *Dentists*. The headings in the Yellow [Pages are] in alphabetical order. You can find the headings by using the g[uide words] at the top of each page.

Use the following section of a page from the Yellow Pages to answer the questions below.

D DIAPERS – DOORS

DIAPER SERVICE

CUDDLES DIAPER SERVICE
  2383 Kings Road, Oakville 555-3457
FAST 'N EASY DIAPER
  211 Open Court, Kingston 555-8976

DISC JOCKEYS

EDWIN CANTRELL
  3190 Ohio Boulevard, Oakville 555-0135
SOUND-A-RAMA
  32 Hoover Road, Oakville 555-4367

DIESEL FUEL

ARTHUR LONG OIL SERVICE
  79 Glenridge Road, Glenmont 555-2894
A. W. RUSSO AND SONS
  1298 Central Avenue, Oakville 555-8776

DOORS

McKEE LUMBER
  11 Grove Street, Oakville 555-7876
O'BRIEN GARAGE DOOR CO.
  1011 Park Place, Adamsville 555-6754

1. What are the guide words on this page of the Yellow Pages? _____
2. Under what heading is Sound-a-Rama listed? _____
3. Which number would you call if you wanted to buy diesel fuel in Oakville? _____
4. What is the address for the O'Brien Garage Door Company? _____

5. What number would you call if you wanted to hire Edwin Cantrell to be a disc jockey at your party? _____

PAST AND PRESENT

Lesson 30   Theme

Reading a Literature Selection

This selection is an old tale from Korea. As you read the story, think about what the storyteller is telling you about kindness.

WORD ATTACK STRATEGIES

■ Hard and Soft g

Many words begin with the letter *g*. Sometimes *g* has a **hard** sound, as in the word *gallon*. Sometimes *g* has a **soft** sound, as in the word *gym*.

Look at the words in the box below. Read them silently. Do you notice how the sound of the letter *g* changes? Usually, the letter *g* has a hard sound when it is followed by the vowel *a, o,* or *u*. The letter *g* has a soft sound when it is followed by the vowel *e, i,* or *y*.

| gentle | gates | golden |
| giant | guide | generously |

1. Read the words in the box again. Underline the words with the hard *g* sound.

■ Adjectives That Compare

Adjectives are words that describe people, places, things, or ideas. The ending *-er* is added to some adjectives to compare two persons, places, things, or ideas. The ending *-est* is added to compare three or more.

| small | smaller | smallest |

Sometimes, you need to change the spelling of an adjective before you add *-er* or *-est*. You may need to make one of the following changes.

Drop final *e*:   large lar**ger** lar**gest**
Change *y* to *i*:   funny funn**ier** funn**iest**
Double final consonant: hot hot**ter** hot**test**

2. Write the comparing forms of the following adjectives.

sad   _____   _____

happy   _____   _____

strange _____   _____

■ Word Clues

When you read, try to figure out the meanings of new words. Use clues in nearby sentences to help you. What clues can help you tell the meaning of the underlined word below?

Each morning, he sailed out to sea and <u>cast</u> his net for fish, throwing the net as far as he could.

The words *throwing the net* can help you figure out that, in this sentence, the word *cast* means "threw."

3. As you read "Obu and the Sea Princess," think about the meanings of the underlined words. Match each word below with its correct meaning.

battered   very confused

grieving   hit hard

bewildered   feeling deep sadness

SKILL FOCUS

■ **Theme**

Do you know the story "The Tortoise and the Hare"? In the story, a turtle and a rabbit have a race. When the race begins, the rabbit hops far ahead. He thinks he is sure to win the race, so he decides to take a short nap. Meanwhile, the turtle crawls slowly on. When the rabbit finally wakes up, it is too late. The turtle is about to cross the finish line and win.

This story has a message for readers. The author is saying, "A slow and steady pace leads to victory." The author might also be giving readers a warning: "Stay alert! Don't be too confident."

The meaning, or message, of a story is called its **theme**. The theme is what the author wants you to learn from the story. Usually, the theme is a message about people or life.

Sometimes the theme of a story is stated directly. One of the story characters, for example, might say what he or she has learned from the events of the story. Usually, however, the reader has to figure out the theme. To do that, look at the whole story. Think about what the author is trying to tell you about life.

The title of a story might give a clue to its theme. In just a few words, the title often tells what the story is about. As you figure out the theme, think about the story title.

Answering the following questions will help you figure out the theme of a story.

- What does the title mean?
- What do the people in the story learn about themselves or others?
- What do the characters learn about life by the end of the story?
- What is the author's message to the reader?

Think back to the story "Thin Ice," on pages 8–9. In that story, Jed rescues his friend Matt. Use the questions at the bottom of the left column to help you figure out a theme of the story.

4. What does the title "Thin Ice" refer to in the story? _____

5. What do you think Jed learns about himself by rescuing Matt? _____

6. What should Matt have learned about life by the end of the story? _____

7. What is the message, or theme, of the story? _____

■ **Strategy Tip** ■

As you read "Obu and the Sea Princess," think about the message that it gives about life. Use the questions on this page to help you figure out the story's theme.

Obu and the Sea Princess

Words to Know

enchanted (en CHANT əd)
magical

transformed (trans FORMD)
changed in form or appearance

compassion (cəm PASH ən)
kindness; sharing the suffering of another

treasure (TREZH ər)
something of great value

Hundreds of years ago, a young Korean fisherman named Obu (ah boo) lived with his mother in a little hut beside the sea. Each morning he sailed out to sea and cast his net for fish, throwing the net as far as he could. Some days, he was lucky and came home with a basketful of fish. Other days, he came home with nothing.

One afternoon, the fisherman caught a giant sea turtle. It was the biggest turtle he had ever seen. "The shell and the meat will bring a high price," Obu thought happily. As he struggled to pull the turtle into the boat, however, Obu began to change his mind. "It's a shame to harm this turtle," he decided. "It may be a thousand years old. Who am I to kill it?" So, in the end, the gentle fisherman let the turtle go.

That night, Obu told his mother about the giant turtle. "You did well to show kindness, my son," said his mother.

A few days later, Obu was out fishing when a storm arose at sea. Obu struggled to reach shore, but the strong winds and huge waves battered his boat. The waves hit the boat so hard that it broke into a dozen pieces. Poor Obu sank beneath the waves.

Under the water, a strange thing happened. Obu saw beautiful towers and bridges. A rainbow of fish—red, green, silver, and gold—swam ahead of him. Soon, he neared an underwater palace surrounded by gates of pearl.

The gates swung open, and a young woman appeared. "Welcome to my palace, Obu," she said. "I am the Sea Princess."

As Obu fell to his knees, the Sea Princess said, "No, don't bow. Come sit beside me." She clapped her hands, and sea creatures appeared. Each had a tray piled high with delicious food. The Sea Princess shared generously with Obu. Each dish was tastier than the last. Obu had never been happier.

Soon, the sea creatures began to make music and sing. Obu and the princess talked and danced. To Obu, the entire palace seemed **enchanted**.

Suddenly, Obu remembered his mother in the world above the waves. She probably thought he had drowned in the storm. How sad she must be! She was probably grieving for him this very minute.

"I must go back to my village," Obu told the Sea Princess. "I must tell my mother that I'm all right. She needs me to take care of her."

"I thought you were happy here," the Sea Princess said.

"Your palace is a wonderful place," replied Obu, "but my home and village are where I must be."

Again and again, the Sea Princess tried to persuade Obu to stay, but Obu's mind was made up.

"Well, then, if you must go," the Sea Princess said, "I will guide you." Suddenly, the princess's hands and feet turned into strong green claws. A hard shell formed on her back. In seconds, the Sea Princess had **transformed** herself into a giant sea turtle!

"Not very long ago," the turtle said, "you showed great **compassion** toward me, Obu. You acted generously toward me, and now I will return your kindness." Taking Obu's hand, she pulled him gently to the surface of the sea.

"I must leave you now," the turtle said, "but take this to remember me by." The turtle handed Obu a golden box. Then the turtle swam beneath the waves.

<u>Bewildered</u>, Obu looked around in confusion. Which way was home? How would he get there? As if in answer, a smaller sea turtle popped its head above the waves. Then another and another appeared. Soon it seemed as if all the turtles in the sea had come to Obu's aid. Together, they formed a long green line stretching far to the east.

Climbing up onto the first turtle's back, Obu started off. The backs of the turtles were like a bridge, and the fisherman jumped lightly from one to the next. Before long, the beach was in sight. Then he could even see his mother and the other villagers standing by the shore.

How happy Obu and his mother were to be together once again! The villagers bowed in respect when they saw how Obu had been saved from the sea.

In his hands, Obu still clutched the golden box. Inside were the finest pearls from the palace of the sea. With this **treasure**, Obu and his mother lived a long and happy life.

Comprehension — Write the answers to the following questions on the lines.

1. Why does Obu let the giant sea turtle go? <ins>Obu let the giant sea turtle go because it was the biggest turtle he had ever seen.</ins>

2. Why does Obu feel he must leave the palace of the Sea Princess? <ins>He feel must leave because he must tell his mother that he all right.</ins>

3. How does Obu return to the beach and his village? <ins>He walks on the back of the smaller turtles.</ins>

Critical Thinking — Write the answers to the following questions. You will have to figure out the answers because they are not directly stated in the selection.

4. What do you know about Obu from his decision to return home? <ins>Obu is kind and loving.</ins>

5. What details show that this story is a folk tale and not a realistic (happen) story? <ins>A turtle can't turn to princess.</ins>

6. If you were in Obu's place, would you return to the village or stay in the palace under the sea? Explain your answer. <ins>If I were in Obu's place, I would return to the village because I want to stay with my famliy.</ins>

Skill Focus — Answer the following question about the story's theme.

7. Think about the theme of the story. Write what you think the story shows about life. If you like, use the questions on page 81 to help you. <ins>Theme: massage, what comes around goes around.</ins>

Reading-Writing Connection — Do you know a story similar to "Obu and the Sea Princess"? On another sheet of paper, write the story you know, or create one.

Lesson 31 Cause and Effect

Reading a Social Studies Selection

The Inca were people who lived in the mountains of South America long ago. In this selection, you will read about how the Inca ruled a huge piece of land.

WORD ATTACK STRATEGIES

■ Hard and Soft *c*

Many words begin with the letter *c*. Sometimes *c* has a **soft** sound, as in *city*. Sometimes *c* has a **hard** sound, as in *coat*.

Look at the words in the box below. Read them silently. Do you notice how the sound of the letter *c* changes? Usually, the letter *c* has a hard sound when it is followed by the vowel *a, o,* or *u*. The letter *c* has a soft sound when it is followed by the vowel *e, i,* or *y*.

calendar	city	cut
cement	corn	center

1. Look again at the words in the box above. Circle the words with the hard *c* sound.

■ Compound Words

Compound words are made from two or more other words. Read the sentence below. Think about the word in dark type.

> People in the territories also had to keep their **storehouses** full of supplies for the empire.

You may not know the word *storehouses*. You do know the word *store* ("put away") and the word *houses*. Think about what these smaller words might mean together. Then you can figure out what *storehouses* are. Storehouses are "houses or buildings in which to store things."

Now look at the words in the next box.

| nearby | guideposts | underground |

2. What two words do you see in each compound word in the box? Draw a line between the two words.

■ Word Clues

As you read about the Inca, you will see some new words. Look for clues to their meanings in nearby sentences.

Read the sentences below. What clues can help you figure out the meaning of the underlined word?

> Powerful monarchs ruled the Inca Empire. These kings lived in Cuzco, the capital city of the empire.

The words *these kings* in the second sentence are clues. They help you guess that *monarchs* is another word for *kings*.

3. As you read "Ruling the Inca Empire," use word clues to figure out the meanings of the underlined words. Then write the correct word in each blank below.

territory   astronomy   irrigated

The Inca ruled a large _____ in South America. They _____ their fields with water brought down from the mountains. They also studied _____ to learn about the sun, moon, and stars.

SKILL FOCUS

■ **Cause and Effect**

Have you ever seen pictures of the damage a hurricane causes? Trees and power lines are knocked down. Roofs blow off houses. Sometimes, neighborhoods are flooded.

The hurricane and the damage have a **cause-and-effect** relationship. The hurricane is the **cause**. The damage is the **effect**. In a cause-and-effect relationship, one thing (the cause) makes another thing (the effect) happen. You have already looked for causes and effects in Lesson 22 of Unit 3. You can practice this important skill again as you read this selection.

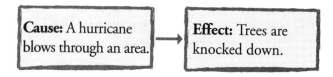

Thinking about causes and effects will help you understand what you read. As you read, ask yourself, "What happened?" The answer will be the effect. Also ask, "Why did it happen?" That will help you find the cause.

Sometimes writers use clue words such as *because*, *so*, and *as a result* to show causes and effects. In the following sentences, for example, the word *so* signals that the writer is about to explain an effect.

> To rule this large area, the Inca needed to travel long distances. **So** they built a network of roads.

Sometimes, however, writers do not use clue words to signal causes and effects. You have to figure out the effect (what happened) and the cause (why it happened) on your own.

Can you figure out the cause and the effect in the following sentences?

> Running the Inca Empire was expensive. The people had to pay taxes to support the empire.

If you ask, "What happened?" the answer is that the people had to pay taxes. This is the effect. If you ask, "Why did it happen?" the answer is that running the empire was expensive. This is the cause.

4. Read each passage below. Then write the cause and the effect in each passage.

> The Inca had no alphabet, so they left no written records of their civilization.

Cause: _____

Effect: _____

> Archaeologists have uncovered their buried cities. These cities help us see how the Inca lived and ruled.

Cause: _____

Effect: _____

■ **Strategy Tip** ■

Look for cause-and-effect relationships as you read "Ruling the Inca Empire." To find an effect, ask yourself, "What happened?" To find a cause, ask yourself, "Why did it happen?" Sometimes, you will see clue words that help you find causes and effects.

Ruling the Inca Empire

Words to Know

empire (EM peyer)
a group of lands ruled by one person

civilization (siv ə lə ZAY shən)
the way of life of a people or nation

archaeologists (ahr kee AHL ə jists)
scientists who study ancient civilizations

conquistadors (kahn KEES tə dorz)
Spanish explorers who captured new lands for Spain during the 1500s

Five hundred years ago, the Inca **Empire** covered the land that is now the countries of Peru, Ecuador, Bolivia, Chile, and Argentina. Powerful monarchs ruled the Inca Empire. These kings lived in Cuzco (KOOS koh), the capital city of the empire.

The Inca had no alphabet, so they left no written records of their **civilization**. We do know about the Inca way of life, however. **Archaeologists** have uncovered their buried cities. These cities help us see how the Inca lived and ruled.

The Inca ruled about 12 million people. How did they rule their empire high in the Andes Mountains?

Roads

The empire was more than 2,500 miles long. To rule this large area, the Inca needed to travel long distances. So they built a network of roads.

Some roads went to the area that is now Chile. Some went to Colombia. The roads went from the Pacific Ocean to the Amazon River.

Inca roads were not rough trails. They were wide and straight. They were probably the best roads in the world at that time. Workers paved the roads with flat stones. They placed stones very close together. Not even a knife blade could fit between the stones. Because the roads were made so well, some of them are still used today.

Special runners traveled through the empire. They carried messages from one city to another. The runners brought orders from the king to people all over the empire. They also brought back news to Cuzco.

Ordinary people used the roads, too. To make travel easier, the builders placed storehouses along the road every 25 miles.

Lesson 31 Cause and Effect 87

Inside the storehouses were beds where travelers could sleep. These were South America's first "rest stops" and "motels."

New Lands

The Inca fought wars with people from nearby lands to add <u>territory</u> to their empire. When the Inca took over new lands, however, they let the people keep their old rulers. These local rulers could stay as long as they did not go against the Inca king. People in the territories also had to keep their storehouses full of supplies for the empire.

The Inca kings tried not to rule their territories by force. A king needs a large army to rule by force, and large armies are expensive. Instead, the Inca rulers helped the people in their territories. The empire became stronger because people in the territories depended on their Inca rulers.

Farming

A well-run empire needs enough food for everyone. So the Inca worked hard at farming. They used <u>astronomy</u> to figure out the right time to plant crops. Astronomy is the study of the sun, moon, and stars.

The Inca could tell when each season started by watching the sky. They built tall stone guideposts to show where the sun would rise at the beginning of each season. These markers were like calendars. When the sun rose at a certain spot, for example, Inca farmers knew that it was spring. They could then plant their crops.

The Inca also <u>irrigated</u> their fields. They brought water down from mountain lakes to help their crops. To do this, they dug canals and underground tunnels to carry the water. Even when there was no rain, their crops of potatoes and corn could still grow.

Working for the Empire

Running the Inca Empire was expensive. The people had to pay taxes to support the empire. Because the Inca did not use money, people paid taxes by working for the empire.

Everyone had to work for the empire a few weeks each year. The people worked on roads and bridges. They built temples and other buildings.

Keeping Records

To rule their empire, the Inca needed to keep track of information. They needed to know how many people were in each city. They needed to know how much food they had stored. They needed to know who had paid taxes. How did the Inca keep track of this information without a written language?

To keep records, the Inca hung strings of different colors and lengths. This set of strings was called a *quipu* (KEE poo).

Each color of string stood for something different. For example, one color stood for people in a village. Another color showed baskets of potatoes. Record keepers tied knots on the strings to show numbers. Each knot near the top of a string stood for 100. Each knot in the middle meant 10. Each knot near the bottom end stood for 1.

The Inca used a *quipu* like this one to keep records.

Temples and Ceremonies

Religion played an important part in the lives of the Inca. The rulers held many religious ceremonies. These ceremonies

Pictured above are the remains of an ancient Inca city in the Andes Mountains called Machu Picchu. It was not discovered until 1911.

included dancing, feasts, games, and songs. People traveled long distances to attend them.

Temples, or religious buildings, were at the center of city life. Inca temples were beautiful. Builders cut each stone to fit perfectly with the others. They used no cement. Cutting these stones took great skill because the Inca had no iron tools.

Gold made the temples special, too. The Inca dug gold from the earth. They melted the gold in clay furnaces. Then they hammered the gold into thin sheets. They used these sheets of gold to cover the outside of many of their temples. They also placed golden ornaments inside the temples.

The End of the Empire

The Inca Empire was well organized. Its kings were good rulers. Even so, this empire lasted only about 100 years.

In 1532, Spanish explorers reached Peru. These **conquistadors** were looking for gold. They also wanted to capture new lands for Spain. The conquistadors killed the ruler of the Inca. Soon, the Spanish took over the empire.

A whole civilization was changed forever, and many of its treasures were lost. Luckily, however, visitors can now see ancient Inca cities such as Machu Picchu, which was uncovered by archaeologists in 1911.

| **Comprehension** | Write the answers to the following questions on the lines. |

1. How did the Inca keep records without a written language? _____
_____

2. How did Inca farmers water their fields during dry times? _____
_____

3. What did the Inca do to make their temples special? _____
_____

| **Critical Thinking** | Write the answers to the following questions. You will have to figure out the answers because they are not directly stated in the selection. |

4. Why do you think the Inca let people in the territories keep their old rulers? _____
_____
_____

5. How do we know so much about Inca roads and temples? _____
_____
_____

| **Skill Focus** | Draw a line to match each cause with its effect. Look for what happened (the effect) and why it happened (the cause). |

Cause

6. The empire was more than 2,500 miles long.

7. Inca roads were very well built.

8. The Inca did not use money.

9. It was too expensive to keep armies in the territories.

Effect

a. People paid their taxes by working for the empire.

b. The Inca helped their territories instead of ruling by force.

c. The empire needed many good roads.

d. Some Inca roads are still used today.

| **Reading-Writing Connection** | Would you like to be an archaeologist who discovers ancient cities? Why or why not? On another sheet of paper, explain your reasons. |

Lesson 32 Making Generalizations

Reading a Science Selection

Have you been in a greenhouse? Did you enjoy its warmth? In this selection, you will learn how our planet is like a greenhouse that may be getting too warm.

WORD ATTACK STRATEGIES

■ Letters *ph* and *gh*

The letters *ph* and *gh* stand for the /f/ sound in some words. These letters can appear at the beginning, in the middle, or at the end of words. The words in the box are from the selection. In each word, the letters *ph* or *gh* stand for the /f/ sound.

tough	graphs	enough
atmosphere	geography	

1. Read the words in the box silently. Circle the letters in each word that spell the /f/ sound.

■ Compound Words

A **compound word** is formed from two or more other words. Some compound words, like *birdhouse,* are written together as one word. Other compounds, such as *post office,* are written as two separate words. A few compounds, like *twenty-one,* use a hyphen between the two words.

Look at the compound words in the box. You will see them again in the selection.

carbon dioxide	all-time	worldwide
greenhouse	rainfall	fossil fuels

2. What two words make up each of the compounds above? Draw a line between the two words in each compound.

■ Word Clues

As you read this selection, try to figure out the meanings of new words. Clues in nearby sentences can help you. What clues, for example, show the meaning of the underlined word below?

> The higher seas could <u>submerge</u> cities along the coast. The cities would then be under water.

If you do not know what *submerge* means, the next sentence gives you a clue. After the cities are submerged, they are under water. *Submerge* means "to place under water."

3. As you read "The Greenhouse Effect," use word clues to figure out the meanings of the underlined words. Then answer *yes* or *no* to each of the following questions based on information in the selection.

Can people <u>adapt</u> to changes in the weather?

_____

Can people <u>predict</u> everything about the future? _____

Should people try to <u>preserve</u> forests?

_____

SKILL FOCUS

■ Making Generalizations

Suppose you had three friends who always studied hard and did well on tests. Your other friends, who did not study, did not do well on tests. Based on these facts, you might say, "Studying hard leads to good grades." This would be a generalization.

A **generalization** is a broad statement that applies to many examples. A generalization shows what the examples or facts have in common. Below are two more examples of generalizations.

> **Many** scientists believe that Earth's climate is getting warmer.

> The increasing amount of carbon dioxide in the atmosphere is **generally** blamed for the warm-up.

Generalizations often contain clue words. The words *generally* and *in general* signal generalizations. Some other common clue words are *all, no, most, many, always, everyone, everywhere, some, often,* and *overall*. These words show that a statement applies to many facts or examples.

Read the following two sentences. Which is a fact? Which is a generalization?

> Three of the hottest years on record occurred during the 1990s.

> Many of the hottest years on record have occurred recently.

The first sentence is a specific fact. The second sentence is a generalization. It applies to many facts and examples.

Be careful when you read generalizations. Not every generalization can be trusted. Some generalizations are faulty. A faulty generalization may not be based on enough facts or examples. It may not make sense.

4. Read the following paragraphs. Underline one sentence in each that is a generalization. Circle the clue word that helped you to identify the generalization.

> The sea ice off Antarctica is shrinking. In Kenya and Colombia, insects are moving into areas that used to be too cool for them. In Alaska, four of the five earliest thaws on record have occurred in the 1990s. In 1999, New York City had its warmest July on record. Everywhere you look, the climate is warming up.

> Most of the predictions about a warmer climate warn of its dangers. Florida and Louisiana will flood. The Sahara Desert will grow larger. Farmers in the Midwest will not be able to raise corn. The Southwest will be so dry that people will have to move away.

■ Strategy Tip ■

As you read "The Greenhouse Effect," look for generalizations. Think about whether the generalizations make sense and whether they are based on enough facts and examples.

The Greenhouse Effect

Words to Know

atmosphere (AT mə sfir)
the layer of gases that surrounds Earth

carbon dioxide (CAR bən deye AHKS eyed)
a colorless, odorless gas that traps heat in the atmosphere

global warming (GLOH bəl WOR ming)
a slow increase of temperatures around the world

evaporation (i VAP ər AY shən)
the process by which a liquid, such as water, is changed to a gas, such as water vapor

What Is the Greenhouse Effect?

The **atmosphere** is a blanket of gases around Earth. It goes up more than 300 miles. Nitrogen and oxygen are the main gases in the atmosphere. These gases make up 99 percent of the total atmosphere.

Carbon dioxide and a few other gases are also part of the atmosphere. They are less than 1 percent of the atmosphere. Still, they are important. These gases trap the sun's heat when it is reflected off Earth, warming the land and oceans. This trapping of heat by gases in the atmosphere is called the greenhouse effect.

In a way, carbon dioxide acts like a car window on a summer day. The glass in the window lets sunlight in. The heat cannot get out, though. So the car gets very hot inside. The glass in a greenhouse acts in the same way to trap heat, which protects plants from the cold. The greenhouse effect makes life on Earth possible. We need carbon dioxide in the atmosphere. Otherwise, Earth's temperature would be below freezing.

Other planets have a greenhouse effect, too. Venus has an atmosphere thick with carbon dioxide. The atmosphere traps so much sunlight that Venus's temperature is about 880°F! Mars has a thin atmosphere. There is only a little carbon dioxide. The temperature on Mars is about −67°F. Most scientists think that this is not warm enough for life.

What Is Global Warming?

During the past 200 years, humans have been adding carbon dioxide to the air. Every time we burn fossil fuels such as coal and gasoline, we put more carbon dioxide into the air. A car, for example, pumps out four tons of carbon dioxide each year!

The factories that people have built also burn fuel and give off carbon dioxide. So

The greenhouse effect occurs when carbon dioxide in the atmosphere traps the sun's heat.

carbon dioxide levels keep increasing. Another activity that leads to rising carbon dioxide levels is the cutting down of forests. Growing trees take carbon dioxide out of the air every day. They use the carbon dioxide to make food. When the trees are cut down, more carbon dioxide stays in the air.

Today, the carbon dioxide level in the atmosphere is at an all-time high. It is about 25 percent higher than it was in 1860. The blanket of gases around Earth is getting thicker.

This steady increase in carbon dioxide will trap more and more heat. Some scientists believe that, as a result, Earth's temperature will rise. Over the last 120 years, some scientists have tracked Earth's average temperature. They have made graphs that show the temperature of Earth has increased about 1°F in the last century. Many scientists believe this warming will soon speed up. An increase of 2°F to 6°F over the next century is possible. This trend is called **global warming**.

Why Is Global Warming a Problem?

A few degrees may not sound like much. Experts generally agree, however, that global warming could have serious effects. Such changes would be greatest near the North Pole and the South Pole. The ice in these areas might melt. This polar ice holds more than 95 percent of the world's fresh water.

Fed by melting ice, the sea level would rise. A rise of several feet could wash away beaches. The higher seas could submerge cities along the coast. The cities would then be under water. Great harm would be done.

Global warming could also cause changes in the weather. Soil, rivers, and lakes could dry up through **evaporation**. As water evaporated, it could form more clouds. Such a change would cause more rain and snow to fall on Earth. However, some areas would get much more rainfall, while others would get less. The amounts would depend on where the winds moved the clouds formed by evaporation.

Some scientists think that the American Midwest would get much less rain. That could turn Midwestern farms into deserts, seriously affecting our food supply.

Changes in the weather could affect plants and animals all over the world. Many animals could adapt to the changes. They could change their way of life. Trees and other plants, however, would have trouble.

Scientists use computers to try to predict what the effects of global warming will be. However, no one can know exactly what will happen next. There are many things that affect our weather, including winds, clouds, oceans, pollution, and geography. Different scientists often make different predictions because there are so many facts to consider and interpret.

What Can We Do?

We must act now to cut the amount of carbon dioxide in the air. To solve the problem, we need to find new sources of energy that do not put carbon dioxide into the air. In the meantime, we can save energy. Burning less gasoline in our cars would keep a great deal of carbon dioxide out of the atmosphere.

We also need to preserve the forests we have now and plant new ones, as well. Trees take large amounts of carbon dioxide out of the atmosphere. They also add oxygen.

Global warming affects us all. It is a worldwide problem. All the countries of the world need to work together to solve it.

| **Comprehension** | Write the answers to the following questions on the lines. |

1. Why are carbon dioxide levels in the atmosphere increasing? _____

2. How has Earth's temperature changed over the last 120 years? _____

3. Why might flooding be a major effect of global warming? _____

| **Critical Thinking** | Write the answers to the following questions. You will have to figure out the answers because they are not directly stated in the selection. |

4. Why do you think the author wrote this article? _____

5. Why will global warming be a difficult problem to solve? _____

6. What can you do in your own community to help solve the problem of global warming?

| **Skill Focus** | On the lines below, write three generalizations from the selection. Circle the clue words that signal each generalization. |

7. Generalization 1: _____
8. Generalization 2: _____
9. Generalization 3: _____

| **Reading–Writing Connection** | Do you agree that people need to act now to stop global warming? On another sheet of paper, explain why or why not. |

Lesson 33 Word Problems

Reading a Mathematics Selection

When you solve word problems, you need to decide which facts are important. Sometimes you may have more information than you need. In this selection, you will learn how to choose the facts you need to solve a word problem.

WORD ATTACK STRATEGIES

■ **Word Clues**

As you read about solving word problems, look for clues to the meanings of new words. For example, what clue in the following sentence can help you figure out the meaning of the underlined word?

> To solve many word problems, you need to focus on, or pay attention to, the facts you need.

You may not know the word *focus*. However, the words *pay attention to* tell you the meaning. To *focus* on a fact means to "pay attention to" it.

As you read "Solving Word Problems That Have Too Much Information," use word clues to figure out the following words. Then fill in the correct word on each blank.

identify   confuse

When you solve a word problem, you must _____ the information you need.

Don't let unneeded information _____ you.

SKILL FOCUS

■ **Word Problems**

Yesterday, milk cost $2.39 a gallon and eggs cost $1.09 a dozen at Ace Market. Today, there is a sale. Eggs cost $0.79 a dozen. Milk is $1.99 a gallon. How much less does milk cost today than yesterday?

The paragraph you have just read is a word problem. A **word problem** is a math problem that is written out in words rather than just in numbers. To solve word problems, you need to use reading and math skills.

Word problems give you the information you need to solve them. Some word problems, however, also contain facts that you do not need. You have to decide which facts you need and which facts you do not.

Look again at the word problem above. What is it asking? The problem asks about the change in the price of milk. So you do not need any of the facts about eggs to solve the problem. When a math problem has facts you do not need, cross them out. That way, they will not confuse you.

> ■ **Strategy Tip** ■
>
> When you read a word problem, think about whether you have more information than you need. If so, cross out the extra information. Then use the five steps in the selection to solve the problem.

Solving Word Problems That Have Too Much Information

Words to Know

disregard (dis ri GARD)
pay no attention to; ignore

unnecessary (un NES ə ser ee)
not needed

To solve many word problems, you need to focus on, or pay attention to, the facts you need. You must **disregard** any facts that are not needed to solve the problem.

Here are the five steps you can use to solve a word problem.

1. Read the problem.

As you read, find the facts in the problem. Underline the question you need to answer.

Mr. Thomas bought his first new pickup truck in 1960 for $3,175. Mr. Thomas's son bought his first new pickup in 1980. It cost $8,150. In 2000, Mr. Thomas's granddaughter bought a new pickup for $17,429. How much less did Mr. Thomas pay for his first pickup truck than his granddaughter paid for hers?

You can put the facts from the problem in a list, like the one below.

Mr. Thomas paid:	$ 3,175
His son paid:	$ 8,150
His granddaughter paid:	$ 17,429

What question does the problem ask? The last sentence gives the question: *How much less did Mr. Thomas pay for his pickup truck than his granddaughter paid for hers?* Now that you know the question, you can <u>identify</u>, or pick out, the facts you need to answer it.

2. Decide how to find the answer.

Notice that the question asks only about Mr. Thomas and his granddaughter. The fact about Mr. Thomas's son is **unnecessary**. Cross out this fact. Otherwise, it might <u>confuse</u> you.

Mr. Thomas paid:	$ 3,175
~~His son paid:~~	~~$ 8,150~~
His granddaughter paid:	$ 17,429

Look again at the last sentence in the problem. The words *how much less* tell you that you need to subtract.

3. Estimate the answer.

An estimate is a good guess. To estimate, first round the numbers in the problem. Then do the math. You can round the truck prices to the nearest $1,000.

$17,000 − $3,000 = $14,000

Your estimate is $14,000.

4. Carry out the plan.

To carry out the plan, use the numbers from the problem. When you are finished, be sure to check your work.

$17,429 − $3,175 = $14,254

5. Read the problem again, and write your final answer.

Check that your answer makes sense. Then you can write the complete answer.

Mr. Thomas paid $14,254 less than his granddaughter did.

To make sense, the answer should be close to your estimate.

Lesson 33 Word Problems 97

| **Comprehension** | Write the answer to the following question on the line. |

1. Why is it a good idea to underline the question you need to answer in a word problem?

_____

| **Critical Thinking** | Write the answer to the following question. You will have to figure out the answer because it is not directly stated in the selection. |

2. Why do you need to decide how to answer the problem before you cross out extra facts?

_____

| **Skill Focus** | Use the five steps to solve the following word problems. Cross out the unnecessary information in each problem. |

3. Read: Mr. Martin bought a house in 1950 for $16,780. He sold it in 1970 for $49,890. The house sold again in 2001 for $189,500. What was the difference between the price Mr. Martin paid and the price for which he sold the house?

Decide: _____

_____

Estimate: _____

Carry Out: _____

Reread/Final Answer: _____

4. Read: Barbara Stevens and her daughter Mae work at the same plastics factory. Mrs. Stevens began work there in 1960, earning $95 a week. Mae went to work at the factory in 1980 for $190 a week. Today, the starting wage is $289 a week. What is the difference between today's starting wage and the starting wage in 1980?

Decide: _____

Estimate: _____

Carry Out: _____

Reread/Final Answer: _____

| **Reading-Writing Connection** | On another sheet of paper, write a word problem with extra facts. Trade papers with a partner, and solve each other's problem. |

Lesson 34 Hard and Soft c and g

The consonant *c* has two sounds: **soft *c***, as in *cent*, or **hard *c***, as in *can*. consonant *g* also has two sounds: **soft *g***, as in *gem*, or **hard *g***, as in *goose*.
How do you know when these letters have a hard sound and when they have a soft sound? Use the following rules as a guide.

Usually, *c* has a hard sound when it is followed by the vowel *a, o,* or *u.*

| catch | could | cut |

Usually, *c* has a soft sound when it is followed by the vowel *e, i,* or *y.*

| cell | city | cycle |

Usually, *g* has a hard sound when it is followed by the vowel *a, o,* or *u.*

| gallon | gold | gut |

Usually, *g* has a soft sound when it is followed by the vowel *e, i,* or *y.*

| gentle | giant | gym |

The words below begin with *c* or *g.* Say each word to yourself. Decide which sound *c* or *g* has. Write *hard* or *soft* on the line.

1. general _____
2. gypsy _____
3. gulf _____
4. computer _____
5. carton _____
6. camera _____
7. ginger _____
8. century _____
9. gallant _____
10. golfer _____
11. current _____
12. cider _____
13. career _____
14. garden _____
15. genius _____
16. gush _____
17. generation _____
18. cedar _____
19. cord _____
20. central _____

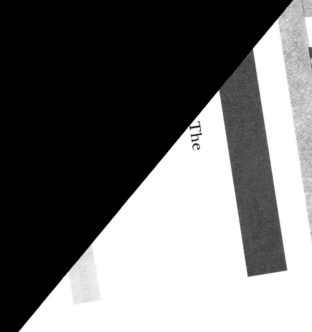

```
                                              = post office
```

... are written with hyphens (-).

twenty + one = twenty-one   up + to + date = up-to-date
father + in + law = father-in-law

Read each sentence below. Underline the compound word.

1. Randy took a jump shot just before the buzzer sounded.
2. The ball hit the backboard and danced around the rim.
3. We looked at the scoreboard and saw that the game was tied.
4. The principal and vice-principal were cheering loudly.
5. The biggest game of the season would be decided in overtime.

Draw a line from each word in Column A to a word in Column B to form a compound word. Write each compound on the line.

	A	B	
6.	tooth	father	_____
7.	paper	ache	_____
8.	grand	conditioner	_____
9.	vice	back	_____
10.	air	president	_____

Lesson 36 Using Parts of a Book

Many books have special parts to help you find information. A **table of contents** is at the beginning of a book. This page lists all the chapters in the book in order. It tells on which page each chapter begins. A table of contents gives you an overview of what is in a book. Using the table of contents, you can find a chapter quickly.

Many books also have an **index** at the back. The index lists all the topics mentioned in the book. The topics are listed in alphabetical order. Next to each topic, you will see the page number or numbers where you can find information on that topic. If you want to see if a book covers a certain topic, check the index.

Below is a sample table of contents.

Below is a sample index.

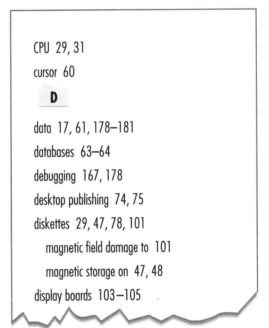

Use the sample table of contents and sample index shown above to answer the following questions.

1. What is the title of Chapter 7? _____

2. Which pages give facts about databases? _____

3. On which page does Chapter 5 begin? _____

4. Which pages should you read to find out about desktop publishing? _____

5. Does the book have a chapter about the Internet? _____

Reading a Diagram

In [scienc]e and social studies books, you will sometimes see **diagrams**. [A diagram is] a drawing that shows how something works or how it changes [over time.]

[A diagram] usually has a **title**. Read the title to find out what the diagram [shows. E]ach part of the diagram has a **label**. Study the labels and pictures [in the] diagram. They may show you the steps of a process or the different [part]s of a machine. Sometimes, a diagram includes **arrows**. The arrows [sh]ow the order in which things happen.

[S]tudy the following diagram. Then use the diagram to answer the questions below.

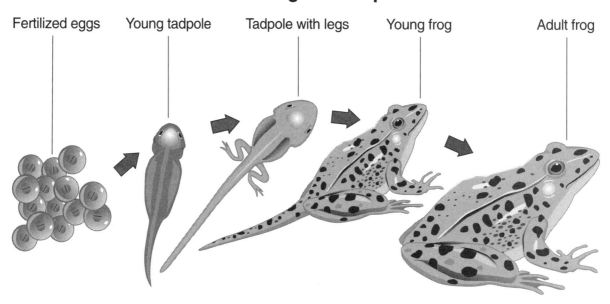

How Frogs Develop

Fertilized eggs • Young tadpole • Tadpole with legs • Young frog • Adult frog

1. What is the title of the diagram? _____

2. What does the diagram show as the first step of frog development? _____

3. What does the diagram show you about the way a young tadpole looks? _____

4. How are a tadpole's legs different from an adult frog's legs? _____

5. How is a young frog different from an adult frog? _____

102 Lesson 37 Reading a Diagram

Lesson 38 Reading Classified A...

Many people place **classified ads** in their local newspa... of the classifieds advertises something different. For ex... ads for cars, apartments, and jobs.

In the "For Sale" classified ads, people advertise things th... Each ad tells about one thing for sale and how much it co... gives an address to write to or a phone number to call for ... information.

Classified ads give a lot of information in a small space, so the... abbreviations. For example, *exc. cond.* is an abbreviation for *exc... condition.* You can usually use context clues to figure out abbrevi...

Use the following classified ads to answer the questions below.

BEDRM SET, Solid oak. Dresser, nightstand, mirror and headboard. Very nice. $850. 555-8642

BEDRM SET, Full-sized Lavon waterbed, dresser, chair. Like new. Delivered. $550. 555-7656

BEDRM SET, Twin Beds w/ Drssr. White. Very pretty. Must sell. $400. 555-8988

BIKE, Girl's Tracker 220, Mountain. Exc. cond. $300. 555-0978

BIKE, Comfortrider, hybrid Street/Mountain. Exc. cond. $325. 555-7431

BIKE, road, Aleki, 18 spd. $100, w/ car rack +$30. 555-1158

BIKE, Mountain. Boys. Small frame. Nds. wrk. $55 or best offer. 555-0987

COMPUTER CDs, More than 25 titles. $15 each. Call for details. 555-8780

COMPUTER DESK, Corner model w/ two-drawer files. $150 for all. 555-4128

---

1. How many ads for bikes are listed? _____
2. Denise is interested in buying the Girl's Tracker 220 mountain bike. What telephone number should she call? _____
3. What type of 18-speed road bike is offered for sale? _____
4. Samantha and her sister are interested in the white bedroom set with twin beds. How much does the set cost? _____
5. What number would you call to find out about buying computer CDs for $15? _____
6. What is the brand name of the waterbed listed in the classified ad? _____
7. In what condition is the boy's mountain bike? How do you know? _____

WORLDS

Conflict and Resolution

Reading a Literature Selection

Do you think people will ever move to other planets? This science-fiction story is about such a move. As you read, think about the problems the characters face.

WORD ATTACK STRATEGIES

■ **Vowel Digraph** *ie*

In a **vowel digraph**, two vowels together can make a long sound, a short sound, or a new sound all their own. The vowel digraph *ie*, for example, can sometimes stand for the long *e* sound you hear in the word *piece*.

1. Read the words below. Underline the words in which the letters *ie* stand for the long *e* sound you hear in the word *piece*.

supplies	chief	believed
briefly	shrieked	replied

■ **Syllables**

Each part of a word in which you can hear a vowel sound is a **syllable**. When you read new words, try dividing them into syllables. Say each syllable. Then put the syllables together to say the whole word.

A two-syllable word with a prefix or suffix is easy to divide into syllables. Divide the word between the prefix and the base word or between the base word and the suffix.

unsafe	un|safe	useful	use|ful

2. Read the following words from the selection. Divide each word into two syllables. Draw a line between the two syllables.

quickly	return	prejudge
unload	farmers	tasteless

■ **Word Clues**

When you read, think about the meanings of the new words you see. Look for details in nearby sentences to help you guess the meanings. What details, for example, can help you figure out the meaning of the underlined word below?

> A shudder of <u>dismay</u> rippled through the crowd. People began to exchange worried glances.

The words *shudder* and *worried glances* are clues. People usually shudder and look worried when they are afraid. So you can tell that the word *dismay* means "fear."

3. As you read "Greetings!," look for clues to the meanings of the underlined words. Then answer *yes* or *no* to each question below.

Are trucks used to <u>transport</u> food? _____

Is Earth free of <u>hostilities</u>? _____

Is an orange <u>edible</u>? _____

SKILL FOCUS

■ **Conflict and Resolution**

Life is full of problems that are hard to solve. Without any problems at all, though, life would be boring. Solving a problem can be very satisfying.

Characters in stories have problems, too. That is why stories are so interesting. The story problem is sometimes called a **conflict**.

Often one character has a conflict with another character. The two characters might disagree with each other or have a fight. Sometimes characters have a conflict with nature. A forest fire, for example, might threaten their lives. Another type of conflict occurs inside the minds of characters, when they cannot decide what they really want or what they should do next.

Characters try to solve their conflicts. The solution to a story's conflict is called the **resolution**. The resolution usually comes at the end of the story.

Read the following paragraph from the story "Greetings!" Think about the conflict that the main character, Lydia, faces.

> Lydia Gomez sat with her head in her hands. Her elbows rested on her torn and dusty pants. All day, she had searched the planet Leonis for food. All she had found were a few tasteless roots. They were barely enough to keep her alive for another day.

From this passage, you can see that Lydia is in conflict with nature. She does not have enough to eat and may starve. As you read the story, you will learn more about this conflict and whether Lydia can resolve it.

4. Often a character faces more than one conflict. Read the following section. What new conflict does Lydia now face? On the lines below, describe the conflict.

> Victor and some of his followers raced off toward the mines. Minutes later, the roar of their machines filled the air. Miners in giant earthmovers were heading toward the alien spacecraft. Others had brought explosives.
>
> "Wait, Victor! Slow down!" Lydia shouted, grabbing the chief miner's arm. "Don't prejudge the situation. We have to find out what's going on first. You can't just blow up this ship!"
>
> "Can't I?" muttered Victor. "That's the only thing Derigans understand." The miners began to unload their explosives.
>
> "Victor, wait!" Lydia pleaded again, grabbing the leader's arm.

Conflict: _____
_____
_____

■ **Strategy Tip** ■

As you read "Greetings!" pay special attention to the conflicts that Lydia faces and how she resolves them at the end of the story.

Lesson 39 Conflict and Resolution

Greetings!

Words to Know

colonists (KAHL ə nists)
people who leave their own country to settle in another land

alien (AY lee ən)
strange; unfamiliar

negotiate (nə GOH shee ayt)
talk something over in order to reach an agreement

humanitarian (hyoo man ə TAIR ee ən)
unselfishly serving the needs of people

Lydia Gomez sat with her head in her hands. Her elbows rested on her torn and dusty pants. All day, she had searched the planet Leonis for food. All she had found were a few tasteless roots. They were barely enough to keep her alive for another day.

How different things had been five years ago! That was when Lydia had first arrived on the planet Leonis. She was one of the planet's first **colonists**. Back then, Leonis had held the promise of a better life.

Leonis had rich supplies of metals. The colonists had quickly dug mines. Every month, spaceships from Earth would transport food and supplies to Leonis. The ships would then return to Earth loaded with gold and other metals.

Then the ships had suddenly stopped coming. No one knew why. Some said that Earth and the planet Deriga had begun hostilities against each other. All Earth's resources were needed to fight the Derigans, they said. Lydia wasn't sure if she believed these stories about a war.

Left alone on a harsh planet, the colonists tried to adapt. Some became farmers. However, the few seeds they had brought with them did not grow well on Leonis. Others hunted for meat or searched for edible plants. They were not sure which plants and animals were safe to eat, though. Hunger had become a way of life.

Wearily, Lydia made her way back to the settlement. Usually everyone would be inside their plastic houses by now. Tonight, however, something was different. The colonists were out in the street. Some were laughing. Others were pointing up and cheering. Lydia hadn't heard such happy sounds in years.

"What is it?" Lydia called out.

"A ship from Earth!" Victor Martinez replied happily. "The first one in four years." Martinez was the chief miner. For the last few years, he hadn't had much to do. What was the use of piling up gold when you are starving?

After briefly circling the settlement, the spaceship touched down on the landing strip. A shudder of dismay rippled through the crowd. People began to exchange worried glances. This was not a familiar green-and-white Earth ship. It was an **alien** craft—silver-colored and shaped like a bug. Near the top of the ship was a strange orange flag.

The colonists watched and waited, but nothing happened. No doors opened. No lights turned on. No radio contact occurred. The ghostly ship just stood there.

"It's the enemy!" Victor finally shouted.

"Yes, the Derigans!" a number of the miners shrieked in agreement.

"Wait!" Lydia cautioned. "That's not the Derigan flag. I've never seen that flag before."

"Then it's a Derigan trick!" Victor replied. "You can't trust the Derigans!"

Victor and some of his followers raced off

toward the mines. Minutes later, the roar of their machines filled the air. Miners in giant earthmovers were heading toward the alien spacecraft. Others had brought explosives.

"Wait, Victor! Slow down!" Lydia shouted, grabbing the chief miner's arm. "Don't prejudge the situation. We have to find out what's going on first. You can't just blow up this ship!"

"Can't I?" muttered Victor. "That's the only thing Derigans understand." The miners began to unload their explosives.

"Victor, wait!" Lydia pleaded again, grabbing the leader's arm. "Let's find out if anyone is inside. Maybe they have news of Earth. We might even **negotiate** with them and have them take us back to Earth."

"Get out of my way," was Victor's answer. He pushed Lydia to the ground.

Horrified, Lydia watched as the miners prepared to destroy the alien craft. There was only one thing to do. Darting across the landing strip, Lydia crawled up onto the tail section of the craft. Balancing carefully, she made her way to the top.

In the distance, Victor's voice boomed. "Don't be a fool, Lydia. We're setting the explosives. You don't have much time."

A faint light pulsed from the top of the ship now. Moving closer, Lydia saw that the light was in the shape of a human hand. Holding her breath, she placed her hand firmly on the light.

All at once, things happened quickly. A loud humming sound filled the ship. Lights flashed. Two cargo doors slid open. Then a recorded message echoed through the night.

"Greetings to the Earth people on Leonis," a voice said. "This is an unmanned **humanitarian** spacecraft from the planet Isobus. We come in peace, bringing food and tools for your survival."

"Don't listen! It's a trick, I say!" Victor's voice shouted from the darkness. The other miners, however, weren't so sure anymore. Food, sacks of grain, and seeds were visible inside the spacecraft's cargo bay. Maybe the alien ship was exactly what it said it was. What should they do? The future of the colony depended on their decision.

Three months later, Lydia walked out toward the hills beyond the settlement. Everywhere she looked, the fields of grain and vegetables were almost ripe. At one field, a farmer waved and hurried over to her. It was Victor.

"I see that you're chief of the farmers now," Lydia said with a smile.

"Thanks to you," Victor replied. "Thanks to you, we have a whole new world to enjoy."

| **Comprehension** | Write the answers to the following questions on the lines. |

1. How did life on Leonis change after the spaceships from Earth stopped coming? _____
_____

2. Why did Lydia rush out and climb up onto the alien spaceship? _____
_____

| **Critical Thinking** | Write the answers to the following questions. You will have to figure out the answers because they are not directly stated in the selection. |

3. At the beginning of the story, the colonists could not grow many crops. Why were their fields doing so well at the end of the story? _____
_____

4. How did Victor Martinez change during the story? _____
_____

5. In your own words, state the theme, or main message, of this story. _____
_____

| **Skill Focus** | Write the answers to the following questions on the lines. |

6. Describe the conflict Lydia had with nature. Tell how the conflict was resolved. _____
_____
_____

7. Describe the conflict Lydia had with another character in the story. Tell how the conflict was resolved. _____
_____
_____

| **Reading-Writing Connection** | On another sheet of paper, write a different ending for the story. Start with the scene in which Lydia climbs onto the spaceship. |

Lesson 40 Main Idea and Details

Reading a Social Studies Selection

What was the world like long ago? We can figure out some things about the ancient world from clues that people have left behind. Still, some mysteries may never be solved. In this selection, you will read about one of these mysteries.

WORD ATTACK STRATEGIES

■ **Vowel Digraph** *oo*

In a **vowel digraph**, two vowels together can make a long sound, a short sound, or a special sound all their own. The vowel digraph *oo*, for example, can stand for the vowel sound you hear in the word *too*. It can also stand for the vowel sound you hear in the word *took*.

1. Read each word in the box below. Listen for the sound made by the letters *oo*. Underline the words in which the letters *oo* stand for the vowel sound you hear in the word *too*.

choose	wooden	looked
proof	stood	smooth

■ **Syllables**

Each part of a word in which you can hear a vowel sound is a **syllable**. When you come to a new word, try dividing it into syllables. Say each syllable. Then put the syllables together until you can say the whole word.

Words with double consonants are easy to divide into syllables. Just divide the word between the two consonants.

happy hap|py	logger log|ger

2. Read the following words from the selection. Divide the words into syllables. Draw a line between the two syllables in each word.

massive	grassy	pillars
million	suggest	support

■ **Word Clues**

As you read the selection, try to figure out the meanings of new words. Sometimes writers will actually give you the definition of a new word. Notice how the writer tells you the meaning of the underlined word in the following sentence.

> This pile of soil grew into a <u>mound</u>, which is a small hill.

Writers often tell you the meaning of special words used in science and social studies. Sometimes the definition appears in the same sentence as the new word. Looking for these definitions will help you understand difficult words.

3. As you read "The Mystery of Stonehenge," look for the definitions of the underlined words. Write the definition of each of the following words on the lines.

trilithons _____

summer solstice _____

eclipses _____

_____

SKILL FOCUS

■ **Main Idea and Details**

When you read an article, you need to find the main idea of each paragraph. The **main idea** is the most important idea in the paragraph. Often, a writer states the main idea in one sentence. The other sentences in the paragraph give **details** that tell more about the main idea.

Often, a writer will not state the main idea directly. It is up to you to figure it out. To do that, think about the details in the paragraph. Most of those details will work together to explain one idea. Ask yourself, "What are these details telling me about the topic?" The answer will be the main idea.

The main idea in the paragraph below is not stated directly.

> The huge, heavy, bluestones came from the mountains of Wales, more than 130 miles away. That is the only place the bluestones exist. The builders might have used boats to carry the stones part of the way. Then they had to drag the stones over land. It took 50 workers to move one stone.

You could use a Main Idea and Details Map like the one below to show the details. Thinking about the details on the map will help you figure out the main idea. All of the details describe how hard it was to get the bluestones of Stonehenge and to move them. You might state the main idea this way: *Getting and moving the huge stones of Stonehenge was a very difficult job.*

4. Read the paragraph below. Think about the details. What do they tell you about the topic? If you like, you can draw a chart to help you figure out the main idea. On the lines below, write the main idea of the paragraph.

> A thousand years ago, some English people believed that King Arthur had ordered the building of Stonehenge. Other people decided that giants must have built the monument. Maybe, some people said, the stones had been there from the beginning of the world.

Main Idea: _Long ago, people made up stories about stonehenge._

MAIN IDEA:		
Detail 1: The stones came from Wales, more than 130 miles away.	**Detail 2:** The builders used boats to carry the stones and dragged them over land.	**Detail 3:** It took 50 workers to move one stone.

■ **Strategy Tip** ■

To help you understand what you read, try to find the main idea. If the main idea is not stated directly, try to figure it out. Think about the details in the paragraph.

The Mystery of Stonehenge

Words to Know

massive (MAS iv)
huge, solid, and heavy

monument (MAHN yə mənt)
any object or site having special historical importance

artifacts (AHR tə fakts)
tools or other objects made by people

observatory (əb ZER və TOR ee)
a place for watching the stars and other heavenly bodies

In a field near the town of Salisbury, England, stands a circle of **massive** stones. The huge stones have stood there for hundreds of years. Even today, thousands of curious visitors come every year to see this mysterious **monument** called Stonehenge and to wonder about it. Why was it built? What purpose did it serve? How did ancient people move these 50-ton stones without horses or wheels?

A thousand years ago, some English people believed that King Arthur had ordered the building of Stonehenge. Other people decided that giants must have built the monument. Maybe, some people said, the stones had been there from the beginning of the world.

In modern times, archaeologists have learned a great deal about Stonehenge. They know that work began 4,000 years ago. For 1,500 years, people added to and changed Stonehenge. Archaeologists know where the stones came from. They also think they know how people moved the stones.

Today, some stones at Stonehenge still stand upright. Others have fallen and lie on their sides on the grassy field. Still others have been carried away. Yet we can imagine how the monument once looked.

The mysterious monument called Stonehenge has fascinated visitors for hundreds of years.

This drawing shows how Stonehenge looked about 3,000 years ago.

An Ancient Burial Site

Stonehenge took hundreds of years to build. Around 2500 B.C., when work first started, it was just a ring-shaped ditch. This ring is still there today. It is more than 300 feet across. As people dug the ring, they piled the soil along the rim. This pile of soil grew into a mound, which is a small hill. Inside the mound, the people dug 56 large, evenly spaced holes. These holes form a circle.

The holes at Stonehenge were filled with ashes. Archaeologists say these ashes came from cremations, the burning of dead bodies. Scientists have found **artifacts** at Stonehenge, too. The ashes and artifacts show that people first used the site for religious services and burials.

The Bluestone Rings

By 2150 B.C., a second stage of building began. At that time, workers raised two circles of bluestones at the center of the mound. They used 82 stones in all. Each stone weighed about 5 tons.

The huge, heavy bluestones came from the mountains of Wales, more than 130 miles away. That is the only place the stones exist. The builders might have used boats to carry the stones part of the way. Then they had to drag the stones over land. It took 50 workers to move one stone.

Why did the people choose these stones and go to so much trouble to get them? There were many other large stones close by. Archaeologists suggest that blue might have been a special color for the people who built Stonehenge. Bluestones are also cool to the touch. Perhaps the people thought the stones had special powers.

A New Building Program

Shortly after the bluestone rings were built, powerful and wealthy chiefs began to rule in what is now England. They brought many different groups of people together under one ruler. These chiefs began a new stage of building at Stonehenge.

Workers dragged in giant stones from about 20 miles away. Some of these stones were 24 feet long and weighed more than 50 tons. The old rings of bluestones were taken down.

These stones are different from the older ones. They are smooth. Hundreds of workers spent years shaping and polishing them. Each one is a neat, rectangular block.

With the new stones, workers built <u>trilithons</u>—two upright stones topped by a horizontal stone called a *lintel*. Five trilithons stood in a horseshoe shape. (There are three left today.) Around the horseshoe, workers built a ring of 30 stones. They capped the ring with a shelf of lintels.

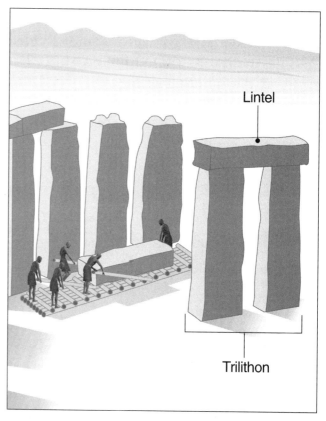

Workers used levers, wooden platforms, and logs to lift the *lintel* that rested on top of two upright stones. The upright stones topped by a lintel are called a *trilithon*.

From the Ground Up

The workers at Stonehenge had only a few simple tools and their bare hands. How did they build a monument that has stood for 4,000 years? Archaeologists think they know the answer.

Teams of men first dragged each stone to its site. Then they dug a pit in which the stone would rest. They did not have shovels, but they may have dug with deer antlers. With ropes, the builders pulled each stone upright into its pit. They used logs to support the stone from behind as they raised it.

To raise a lintel, the workers first slid the stone onto a wooden platform. Then they used levers to raise the platform and stone. A lever is a simple machine like a crowbar. Workers place one end of the bar under the object they want to lift. Then they push down on the other end to raise the object.

As the platform rose, workers placed logs underneath to support it. Slowly, they raised the platform to the top of the pillars—about 30 feet off the ground. Then the workers edged the lintel off the platform and onto the pillars.

Later Developments

Later, workers reset the old bluestones at Stonehenge. This time the stones formed a smaller circle within the large horseshoe of polished stones. Later still, workers rearranged the bluestones into another horseshoe. By 1100 B.C., workers had finished a roadway leading to Stonehenge. This was the last work done there.

All told, many thousands of people worked on Stonehenge. The work went on for more than a thousand years. What was the purpose of this great effort?

An Observatory in Stone?

Many experts think Stonehenge was more than a burial site. They believe it was a special kind of calendar. The people of ancient England did not have clocks or paper calendars. By lining up stones with the position of the sun or moon, however, they could keep track of the seasons. The people who built Stonehenge were farmers. They needed to know when to plant and harvest their crops.

Just outside the monument entrance stands the Heel Stone. On the summer solstice, the longest day of the year, the first rays of the rising sun hit the top of the Heel Stone. A person standing at the center of the circle can see this.

The stones also line up in a special way with the winter solstice, the year's shortest day. On that day, a person at the entrance can look into the circle and see the setting sun between the stones of a certain trilithon.

Some archeologists claim that Stonehenge was more than a calendar. They say the stones and holes formed an **observatory** for watching the moon and stars. The ancient Britons may even have used it to predict eclipses—those rare events when sunlight or moonlight is blocked from Earth.

Other archaeologists disagree, saying that there is not enough proof for these claims. They think Stonehenge was used for religious purposes only.

The people who built Stonehenge had no written language. They left no records telling why they built this amazing monument. This lack of information adds to the site's fascination.

Today, more than a million people visit Stonehenge every year. Meanwhile, scientists continue to explore the site for answers. Perhaps, someday, the mystery of Stonehenge will be solved.

| **Comprehension** | Write the answers to the following questions on the lines. |

1. What beliefs did English people have a thousand years ago about the mystery of Stonehenge? _A thousand years ago, some English people believed that King Arthur had ordered the building of Stonehenge._

2. How were the first stones used at Stonehenge different from the stones brought there later? _The first stones used w_____

3. What are three possible ways that people might have used Stonehenge in ancient times? _____

| **Critical Thinking** | Write the answers to the following questions. You will have to figure out the answers because they are not directly stated in the selection. |

4. How can you tell that Stonehenge must have been a very important monument to the early Britons? _____

5. Do you think we will ever know for sure why Stonehenge was built? Why or why not? _____

| **Skill Focus** | Read the following paragraph from the selection. Think about the main idea that the details describe. Write the main idea on the line. |

Teams of men first dragged each stone to its site. Then they dug a pit in which the stone would rest. They did not have shovels, but they may have dug with deer antlers. With ropes, the builders pulled each stone upright into its pit. They used logs to support the stone from behind as they raised it.

Main Idea: _____

| **Reading-Writing Connection** | On another sheet of paper, describe a monument you would like to build. Explain the monument's purpose and how you would build it. |

Lesson 41 Sequence of Events

Reading a Science Selection

Have you ever seen an eagle or a wolf? In this selection, you will learn what scientists are doing to make sure that these and other animals survive.

WORD ATTACK STRATEGIES

■ Diphthongs *oi, oy, ou,* and *ow*

A **diphthong** is made up of two vowels that blend together to form one sound. Say the words *boil* and *boy*. The diphthongs *oi* and *oy* stand for the same sound. When this sound is at the beginning or in the middle of a word, it is usually spelled *oi*. At the end of a word, it is usually spelled *oy*.

| poisoned | joining | enjoy |

Now say *loud* and *town*. The letters *ou* and *ow* are sometimes diphthongs that stand for the same sound.

| tower | proudly | now | out |

1. Read the words in the two boxes above. Underline the diphthong in each word.

■ Syllables

A **syllable** is a word or part of a word. Each part of a word in which you hear a vowel sound is a syllable. Dividing a word into syllables will help you say the word correctly.

Compound words are easy to divide into syllables. Each of the smaller words in the compound is usually one syllable.

2. Read the following words from the selection. Each has two syllables. Draw a line between the syllables.

| wingspan | offspring | widespread |

■ Word Clues

As you read the selection, use context clues to help you figure out new words. What clues can help you guess the meaning of the word *captivity* in the following passage?

> One way is to breed these animals in captivity—in zoos or wildlife stations. Later, scientists release the animals into the wild.

If you don't know what *captivity* means, the clue *in zoos or wildlife stations* should help you. You know that zoos are places in which wild animals are kept in cages or other small spaces. The second sentence, which is about releasing the animals into the wild, also helps you figure out that *captivity* means "the condition of being held in a confined space."

3. As you read "Helping Endangered Animals Survive," try to figure out the meanings of the underlined words. Then fill in the correct word to fit each definition below.

| inherited | wingspan | recaptured |

_____ caught again

_____ distance from the tip of one wing to the tip of the other wing

_____ received from one's parents

SKILL FOCUS

■ **Sequence of Events**

Suppose you wanted to tell a friend about a trip you took or a party you attended. You would probably begin by telling the first thing that happened. Then you would tell what happened next, what happened after that, and so on. Telling the events in time order would help your friend understand them better.

Writers also explain events in the order in which they happened so that you can understand them. That order is called the **sequence of events**. One way to identify the sequence of events is to ask yourself questions such as "What happened first?" "What happened next?" "What happened at the end?"

Writers often use time-clue words to show the sequence of events. In some articles, dates are important time clues. Look for clues such as *in 1992, by August,* or *on Friday.* Other time clues include words such as *first, next, later, soon,* and *eventually.*

Read the following paragraph. The time-clue words appear in dark type.

> The bald eagle is the national bird of the United States. **Long ago**, 100,000 bald eagles flew proudly over the land. **Then** people cut down woodlands, and eagles lost their habitat. **Later**, many eagles were poisoned by chemicals. **By the 1960s**, there were only a few hundred eagles left.

Sometimes you can use a Sequence Chart like the one at the top of the next column to list events in time order. The first event in the paragraph about the bald eagle is listed on the Sequence Chart.

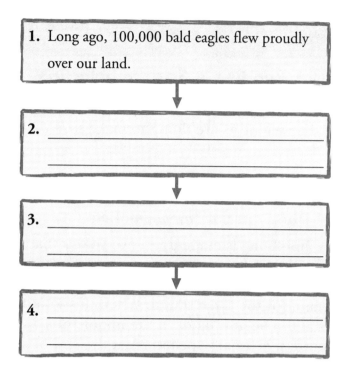

1. Long ago, 100,000 bald eagles flew proudly over our land.

2. _____

3. _____

4. _____

4. Fill in the rest of the Sequence Chart using details from the paragraph about the bald eagle

■ Strategy Tip ■

As you read, think about the sequence of events. Ask yourself questions such as "What happened first?" and "What happened next?" Look for time-clue words to help you figure out the order in which events happened.

Helping Endangered Animals Survive

Words to Know

extinction (ək STINGK shən)
coming to an end; wiping out

species (SPEE sheez)
a group of animals that share certain traits

habitat (HAB ə tat)
a place where an animal lives naturally

endangered (en DAYN jərd)
in danger; likely to become extinct

In the United States, many animals face **extinction**. Luckily, scientists and the U.S. government are joining together to keep some of these animals from dying out. One way is to breed these animals in captivity—in zoos or wildlife stations. Later, scientists release the animals into the wild. Scientists have already helped many **species** this way.

Bald Eagles Flying High

The bald eagle is the national bird of the United States. Long ago, 100,000 bald eagles flew proudly over the land. Then people cut down woodlands, and eagles lost their **habitat**. Later, many eagles were poisoned by chemicals. By the 1960s, there were only a few hundred eagles left.

In 1973, the U.S. government labeled bald eagles an **endangered** species. The government began a program to help these birds survive.

Scientists have also been taking other special steps to help bald eagles. First, scientists take baby eagles from their nests. They place the chicks in cages high in trees or towers. For the first few months, the chicks never see people. A machine lifts food up to their cages.

After 12 weeks, the young eagles grow feathers. Scientists open the cages and let the eagles out. The eagles begin to fly. When they are 6 months old, the birds enjoy soaring long distances. They learn to find food. Finally, scientists set the eagles free in wild areas.

During the 1980s and 1990s, the number of bald eagles grew. By the year 2000, there were more than 4,000 pairs of bald eagles in the United States. Someday, bald eagles may be taken off the endangered list.

The Red Wolf's Return

Red wolves once roamed the United States from the Atlantic coast to Texas. They lived as far north as the Ohio Valley.

Hunters and farmers thought the wolves were pests. They thought the wolves were a danger to farm animals and people, so they hunted the wolves. Soon, they had killed almost all of the red wolves. By 1973, there were only 17 red wolves left. Scientists decided to save them. So they trapped the 17 wolves. In captivity, the number of red wolves steadily rose.

After the number of wolves in captivity had increased, the scientists decided to put some of the wolves back into their

old habitats. The Great Smoky Mountains in Tennessee, for example, had once been a habitat for red wolves. However, the last wolves there had died out in 1905. In 1991, scientists decided to put red wolves back into the Great Smoky Mountains.

Before they relocated the wolves, the scientists worked with people in Tennessee. They told the people about how wolves lived. People often fear wolves until they know the facts about them.

In 1991, scientists brought two families of wolves to the Great Smoky Mountains. At first, they kept the wolves in pens. That way, the wolves could get used to their new home. Then scientists set the wolves free. They watched the animals closely. Later, they brought more wolves to the Great Smoky Mountains.

Scientists have also brought red wolves to North Carolina. About 400 red wolves now live in zoos and in the wild.

New Blood for Florida Panthers

The Florida panther is a type of mountain lion. It is another endangered animal. Florida panthers were once widespread. As more people moved to Florida, however, the panthers lost their habitat. By 1995, there were only 30 Florida panthers left.

Florida panthers also had health problems. Many had weak hearts. Others could not fight off sickness. The offspring of Florida panthers inherited these problems from their parents.

Scientists decided that Florida panthers needed "new blood." In 1995, they trapped eight female panthers in Texas. They set these panthers free in Florida.

The new panthers wore radio collars. That way, scientists could keep track of them. After a while, the Texas panthers had kittens in Florida. Soon, their young will be having kittens. Scientists hope these panthers will be healthier.

Flight of the Condor

The California condor has a 10-foot wingspan, which is the distance from the tip of one wing to the tip of the other wing. It is the largest bird in the United States. It has lived on Earth since ancient times. Guns and poison, however, brought condors close to extinction. By 1987, there were only a few California condors left in the wild.

Scientists caught the remaining birds and placed them in zoos. There, the condors began to breed. In a few years, there were more than 50 birds.

In 1992, scientists set some of the condors free. The birds were soon gliding over the California mountains. In 1996, scientists let out six more condors near the Grand Canyon. There had not been any condors in Arizona since 1924.

So far, scientists have set more than 45 condors free. To help the birds, scientists have put out food for them. Even so, 17 of the condors have died. Another six had to be recaptured because they were not doing well in the wild. Scientists took them back to zoos.

Saving species such as the bald eagle, the red wolf, the Florida panther, and the California condor from extinction is hard work. Still, most people feel that it is important. Many animals have become endangered because of what people did to them or to their habitats. Now it is up to people to help save these animals.

| **Comprehension** | Write the answers to the following questions on the lines. |

1. What caused the Florida panthers to become endangered? _____

_____

2. Why did the number of bald eagles in the United States increase during the 1980s and

1990s? _____

_____

3. How did scientists save the red wolf? _____

_____

| **Critical Thinking** | Write the answer to the following question. You will have to figure out the answer because it is not directly stated in the selection. |

4. Why might some people disagree with the idea that endangered species must be saved?

_____

_____

| **Skill Focus** | Look back at the section about the bald eagles on page 117. Write the sequence of events that happen when scientists save them. |

1. _____

2. _____

3. _____

4. _____

| **Reading-Writing Connection** | On another sheet of paper, tell why you think that one particular kind of animal should never become extinct. |

Lesson 41 Sequence of Events 119

Lesson 42 Reading Mathematical Terms

Reading a Mathematics Selection

What do you think of when you hear the word *point*? What about the word *line*? In this selection, you will learn about the mathematical meanings of these words.

WORD ATTACK STRATEGIES

■ **Word Clues**

As you read about points and lines, you will see some new words. Look for clues to their meanings in nearby sentences.

Read the following sentences. What clues help you figure out the underlined word?

> In math, a point has a position, but it has no <u>dimensions</u>. That means that it has no size. It cannot be measured or even seen.

You may not know what *dimensions* means. The nearby sentences, however, tell you that something without dimensions has no size or measurements. *Dimensions* must be "the measurements that give an object its size."

As you read "Points and Lines," use word clues to figure out the meanings of the underlined words. Write each word's meaning on the lines below.

invisible _____

infinite _____

SKILL FOCUS

■ **Reading Mathematical Terms**

Certain everyday words have special meanings in math. To understand math, you will need to know these meanings. Take, for example, the word *point*. You may think of a point as the tip of a pencil. In math, however, a point cannot be seen at all. It has no dimensions or size.

Another word with a special math meaning is *line*. In everyday life, one meaning of the word *line* is "a group of people waiting to do something." In math, however, a *line* is "an endless number of points placed next to each other." A line has no beginning or end.

	Everyday Meaning	Math Meaning
Point	tip of a pencil	a position with no dimensions
Line	group of people waiting	an endless number of points placed next to each other

Math lessons often include diagrams and symbols to help you understand new words or terms. As you read about points and lines, pay special attention to the diagrams.

■ **Strategy Tip** ■

When you study math, make sure you understand exactly what each new term means. In that way, you will understand the ideas and terms that follow it.

---

120   Lesson 42 Reading Mathematical Terms

Points and Lines

Words to Know

intersect (in tər SEKT)
to cut across or through something

perpendicular (per pən DIK yoo lər)
forming square corners to each other

parallel (PAR ə lel)
being an equal distance apart at every point; not intersecting

In math, the words *point* and *line* have special meanings. In math, a point has a position, but it has no dimensions. That means that it has no size. It cannot be measured or even seen. Even though a point is really invisible, we show its position on paper by using a dot. The dot is named with a capital letter. This is the symbol for point *A*.

•A

A line is many, many points placed next to each other. When a line is drawn, it looks as if it has a beginning and an end. A line is, however, infinite. It goes on forever. The arrows on the line show this.

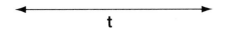

A line can be named with a small letter. Above, for example, is line *t*.

A line can also be named by telling the names of any two points on the line. Capital letters are used to name the two points on the line. These two points can be placed anywhere on the line. Below is a diagram of line *AB*.

When two lines cross, we say that they **intersect**. Two lines intersect at a point. The diagram at the top of the next column shows line *x* and line *y* intersecting at point *O*.

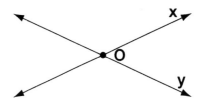

Two lines can intersect and form square corners. Such lines are **perpendicular** to each other. In the following diagram, line *t* and line *v* are perpendicular to each other.

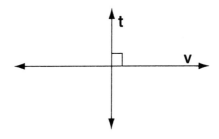

Sometimes two lines never intersect. The distance between them is always the same. When two lines never intersect and go in the same direction, they are said to be **parallel**. In the diagram below, line *a* is parallel to line *b*.

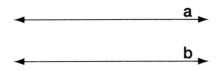

You will use what you have learned about points and lines when you study a type of math called geometry. In geometry, you will learn how points and lines form triangles, rectangles, squares, and other shapes.

Lesson 42 Reading Mathematical Terms **121**

Comprehension — Write a meaning for each of the following terms on the lines.

1. intersecting lines: _____

   parallel lines: _____

   perpendicular lines: _____

Critical Thinking — Write the answer to the following question. You will have to figure out the answer because it is not directly stated in the selection.

2. Look at the following diagram. On the lines next to it, describe what you see.

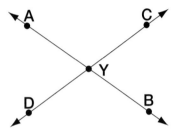

_____

_____

_____

Skill Focus — Draw each of the following.

3. Draw a line. Draw two points anywhere on the line. Label the points X and Y.

5. Draw a line. Label it line p. Now draw a line that is perpendicular to line p. Label the second line s.

4. Draw two parallel lines. Label one line m. Label the other line n.

Reading–Writing Connection — On another sheet of paper, draw something around you that has parallel lines. Then draw something that has perpendicular lines.

Lesson 43 Vowel Digraphs

In a **vowel digraph**, two vowels together can stand for a long sound, a short sound, or a special new sound.

The digraph *ie* can stand for the long *e* vowel sound you hear in *piece*.

| sh<u>ie</u>ld | bel<u>ie</u>f | th<u>ie</u>f |

1. Circle the words below in which the digraph *ie* has the same vowel sound you hear in *piece*.

| pie | believe | fried | grief | chief |
| dried | niece | achieve | died | shriek |

The vowel digraph *oo* can stand for the vowel sound you hear in *moon*.

| r<u>oo</u>m | t<u>oo</u> | n<u>oo</u>n |

The vowel digraph *oo* can also stand for the vowel sound you hear in *look*.

| c<u>oo</u>k | st<u>oo</u>d | h<u>oo</u>k |

2. Each word below has the digraph *oo*. Circle the words in which the digraph stands for the same vowel sound you hear in *moon*.

| book | proof | wood | tooth | shook |
| hood | food | balloon | brook | rooster |

Read each of the following sentences. Underline the words with the digraph *ie* sound you hear in *piece*. Circle the words with the digraph *oo* sound you hear in *moon*.

3. A hot-air balloon landed in the field near a brook where we were fishing.

4. My friends and I looked up and shrieked when we saw it.

5. The balloonists believed they were in Oakville, and we tried to explain their mistake.

6. They left as soon as the chief of police told them they were actually in Elmview.

7. We watched in relief as they untied their craft and zoomed back into the air.

Lesson 44 Diphthongs

A **diphthong** is made of two vowels that form one sound.

Say the words *boil* and *boy* to yourself. Listen to their vowel sound. The letters *oi* and *oy* are diphthongs that have the same sound. When this sound appears at the beginning or in the middle of a word, it is usually spelled *oi*. When it appears at the end of a word, it is usually spelled *oy*, as in *enjoy*.

Read each of the following sentences. Underline the word that has the vowel sound you hear in the words *boil* and *boy*.

1. It is always a joy to plant a garden and watch it grow.
2. Today, I dug up the soil to plant vegetables.
3. My old, rusty shovel uncovered the dark, moist earth.
4. Tonya and Troy came over and asked what I was doing.
5. At one point, I had to dig out a rock.
6. Near it, I found an old plastic toy I had played with long ago.
7. Too bad it wasn't a golden coin or an arrowhead.

Now say the words *out* and *cow*. Listen to their vowel sound. The letters *ou* and *ow* are sometimes diphthongs that have the same vowel sound.

Read each of the following sentences. Underline the words that have the same vowel sound you hear in the words *out* and *cow*. Each sentence has at least two words with this diphthong.

8. High in an old oak tree, a brown owl enjoys the summer evening.
9. From its branch, it looks down waiting for a mouse.
10. Its mouth has a sharp beak that could snap quickly, and the feathers on its head look like a crown.
11. Its tree is its own special tower; from there, it can see the countryside for miles around.
12. How proudly it hoots its loud "Hoo, Hoo."
13. Soon, without a sound, it has spread its soft wings and flown south.
14. "Has it gone to take a tour of town?" I wonder as I wait here on the ground.

Lesson 45 Syllables

Each part of a word in which you can hear a vowel sound is a **syllable**. Dividing words into syllables will help you say them. Pronounce each syllable until you can say the whole word. Here are three rules for dividing words into syllables.

Rule 1: Many words have a prefix or a suffix. Divide the word between the prefix and the base word or between the base word and the suffix.

| redo | re do | hopeful | hope ful | quietly | quiet ly |

Rule 2: Many words have double consonants. Divide these words into two syllables between the double consonants.

| butter | but ter | slipper | slip per | lettuce | let tuce |

Rule 3: Many compound words are made up of two short words. These compounds often have just two syllables. Divide a compound word into syllables by separating it between the two words.

| classroom | class room | rowboat | row boat | popcorn | pop corn |

Divide the following words into syllables. Write each syllable separately on the line to the right of the word.

1. follow _____
2. notebook _____
3. rabbit _____
4. rewrite _____
5. careless _____
6. slowly _____
7. tennis _____
8. softball _____
9. precook _____
10. flutter _____
11. bigger _____
12. ladder _____
13. windshield _____
14. untrue _____
15. backpack _____
16. background _____
17. mammal _____
18. goodness _____
19. bookcase _____
20. tasteful _____

Lesson 46 Reading a Dictionary Entry

A **dictionary entry** is a word and all the information listed about it in a dictionary. The **entry word** is printed in dark type. If the entry word has more than one syllable, the word is divided into syllables.

The entry word is followed by a **respelling** of the word. The respelling shows you how to say the word.

A part-of-speech label follows the respelling. The labels are as follows: *adj.* for adjective, *adv.* for adverb, *conj.* for conjunction, *interj.* for interjection, *n.* for noun, *prep.* for preposition, *pron.* for pronoun, and *v.* for verb.

The meanings of an entry word are grouped by their part of speech. For example, many words can be used as either verbs or nouns. The entry usually groups all the verb meanings together and all the noun meanings together. Each meaning is numbered. After some meanings, the dictionary may give an example of how to use the word in a sentence.

Use the following dictionary entry to answer the questions below. Write your answers on the lines.

> **ar·ray** (ə rā′) *n.* **1** proper order; regular arrangement: *The troops marched in battle array.* **2** display of persons or things: *The store had a beautiful array of jewelry.* **3** military force; soldiers **4** clothes, especially for a special occasion **5** in math, an arrangement of numbers in rows and columns ♦ *v.* **1** put in order for some purpose: array soldiers for battle **2** dress in fine clothes

1. What is the entry word for this entry? _____

2. How many syllables does the entry word have? _____

3. Write the respelling of the entry word. _____

4. How many noun meanings are listed for the entry word? _____

5. How many verb meanings are listed for the entry word? _____

6. Which of the noun meanings of the entry word is used in the following sentence? An array of beautiful paintings filled the room. _____

7. Which verb meaning of the entry word is used in the following sentence? The bride was arrayed in a long, white gown. _____

Lesson 47 Reading a Food Label

Each box, jar, or can in a supermarket has a **food label**. Food labels tell you important facts about the foods you buy.

A food label gives the weight of the product. The label also lists the ingredients, which are what the product is made from. Ingredients are listed in order from the largest amount to the smallest amount.

Most food labels also tell how many servings are in the container. In addition, the label tells how many calories are in each serving and how many of those calories are fat calories. Finally, the label gives facts about the vitamins and minerals the food provides. The label tells what percentage of the nutrients you need every day are in each serving.

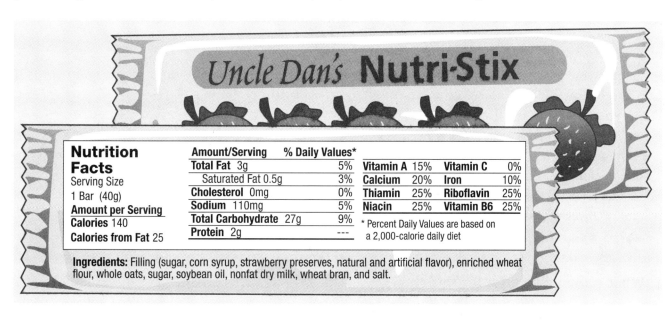

Use the facts on the label shown above to answer each of the following questions. Write your answers on the lines.

1. How much does each bar of Uncle Dan's Nutri-Stix weigh? _____

2. How many calories does one serving of Nutri-Stix contain? _____

3. Could a person on a low-cholesterol diet eat the bars? How do you know? _____
_____

4. Each bar has a fruit filling. What is the main ingredient of this filling? _____

5. How much of your daily need for calcium does one bar provide? _____

6. What type of flour is used in the bar? _____

Word Clues

The following words are treated as context clue words in the lessons indicated. Each lesson provides instruction in a particular context clue type and includes an activity that requires you to use context clues to find word meanings. Word clues appear in the literature, social studies, and science selections and are underlined or footnoted.

Word	Lesson
adapt	32
astronomy	31
atmosphere	22
bank	1
battered	30
bewildered	30
budget	13
cautiously	1
collapsed	20
confessed	10
confuse	33
contributed	21
damage	3
decide	4
distance	23
dragged	1
eclipses	40
edible	39
efficient	12
expensive	12
fabulous	2
fibers	11
gravity	22
grieving	30
hostilities	9
identify	10, 33
impressed	21
infinite	42
inherited	41
invisible	42
irrigated	31
modules	22
mulch	11
perilous	20
plunged	20
praised	21
predict	32
preserve	32
recaptured	41
refused	2
reward	10
rotate	3
savings	13
shred	11
submerged	3
subtract	4
summer solstice	40
sustainable	12
territory	31
transport	39
traveled	2
trilithon	40
units	23
wingspan	41

Words to Know

In lessons that feature literature, social studies, science, or mathematics selections, words that are unique to the content and whose meanings are important in the selection are treated as concept words. These words appear in boldface type and are often followed by a phonetic respelling and a definition.

Word	Lesson
afraid	1
air pollution	12
alien	39
archaeologists	31
artifacts	40
astronauts	22
atmosphere	32
biodegradable	11
carbon dioxide	32
carry out	4
civilization	31
colonists	39
compassion	30
conquistadors	31
course	3
court	2
criminal	10
dangerous	1
delay	20
disguise	10
disregard	33
emergency	20
empire	31
enchanted	30
endangered	41
enemy	21
evaporation	32
evidence	10
extinction	41
eye wall	3
fossil fuels	12
generator	12
global warming	32
habitat	41
hero	1
humanitarian	39
hurricanes	3
incinerators	11
intersect	42
invaded	21
kilometer	23
landfill	11
massive	40
meter	23
military	21
monument	40
negotiate	39
observatory	40
orbits	22
original price	13
parallel	42
passengers	20
percent	13
perpendicular	42
recycling	11
reservation	21
round	4
satellite	22
schedule	20
shortcut	1
Silk Road	2
solar power	12
species	41
storm surge	3
telescope	22
trade	2
transformed	30
treasure	30
unnecessary	33
voyage	2
witness	10